When Oregon National G
killed by an improvised ex[
hurled into a harsh and u.
*Branch*, David's mother, Marilyn, unflinchingly describes her harrowing
journey through this bleak terrain. She grapples with a sense of paralysis,
widespread insensitivity, and physical pain. But she also comes to discern
signs of the Divine, and the recognition that God was speaking to her. "I
see your pain," she hears, "and I am with you." Her book is a powerful
tribute to David and to her family's resilience in the wake of a grievous loss.

**Mike Francis**, reporter, *The Oregonian*

More than memoir, *Empty Branch* is a roadmap to God. This story tore at
my heart, at the very core of me, and drew me into the Weisenburg's loving
circle of family and friends. Lyrical in its lament, affecting in its honesty,
*Empty Branch* is a tender tale between a mother and her son, between a
woman and her God, between a Gold Star mother and her nation.

**Karen Spears Zacharias**, Gold Star daughter and author of *Christian Bend*

I've had the privilege of knowing Marilyn first as her pastor and also as her
friend. Having watched her and her husband, Jim, walk the dark journey
of loss, I'm grateful she is sharing her story with the world. Marilyn writes
with beautiful words and a mother's nurturing love. She helps us see that
in our deepest pain there is the hidden gift called lament. God, for reasons
that I still find mysterious, reveals this gift in our darkest moments, and
Marilyn helps us discover the healing power that the practice of lament
can have on us. This book vulnerably invites us into Marilyn's inner life,
her deep loss and dark nights, and how lament lead her to a hopeful dawn.
If you know someone who is grieving you will want to give them this book.

**Rick McKinley**, Lead Pastor at Imago Dei Community (Portland, Oregon)
Author of *This Beautiful Mess* and *Answer to Our Cry*

Like so many of us who suffer the loss of a loved one, Marilyn was left
questioning if she would ever experience joy again. Her bold, honest account
of loss and redemption proves the immense power of peer connection on
the journey to find healing and a new normal. She shows how her passion to

honor her son's life of selfless service and her willingness to welcome God's grace has provided her the ultimate comfort in the face of profound loss.

**Bonnie Carroll**, president and founder of Tragedy Assistance Program for Survivors (TAPS) and recipient of the Presidential Medal of Freedom

Though her poignant story of the loss of her son during his military service, Marilyn invites her readers to journey into the tension of holding space for grief and the rollercoaster of emotions one encounters. Her words will give readers permission to step into the messiness of lament and "let it have its way with you." Do not be afraid . . . you too may end up discovering a Creator who weeps with you and generously offers the healing balm of His grace and mercy.

**Tara Shepherd Brown**, friend and advocate for creatives, founder and owner of With Creatives

*Empty Branch* is a beautifully told story of one mother's journey through grief after her son was killed in Iraq. With grace, Marilyn Weisenburg shares her intense pain that, in time, gives way to hope, ongoing healing, and finally a chance to care for others on the same road. Throughout the telling, however, Marilyn keeps her writing real and heartfelt. Hers is an honest rendition of sorrow and survival after devastating loss. Every American should read Marilyn's story—we need to know the sacrifices of our gold-star families.

**Leslie Gould**, bestselling and Christy award-winning author

It has been a tremendous honor to journey alongside Marilyn in her healing. On each page of this book I see evidence of her courage, spiritual tenacity, and enormous capacity for love. Few people are willing to walk this rugged path through the inner landscape of heartache. In her honest, poignant narrative, Marilyn articulates the way of suffering as only one well acquainted with grief can. If you have experienced great loss and are tired of clichés and simple answers about your pain, this book will be a *lifeline*. With warmth and kindness on every page, she speaks from the canyon of loss about the tension between the reality of death and the hope of the resurrection.

**Cindy Brosh**, LPC, LMHC

*Finding Hope Through Lament* is an excellent subtitle for this mesmerizing memoir of a family nightmare—the knock at the front door—that relentlessly haunting scene that would replay over and over again in her mind. Marilyn does a remarkable job of drawing the reader into her story in a way that enables readers to feel the emotion alongside understanding multiple facets of lament. Marilyn's grueling honesty in her disorientation touches a place in the reader that encourages further navigation in life's devastating tragedies and losses. "Finding My Voice," "Connection," "Family"—hope slowly surfaces in a journey none would solicit, yet too often arrives at our front door.

**Bev Hislop**, D.Min.
Author of *Shepherding a Woman's Heart* and *Shepherding Women in Pain*
Professor of Pastoral Care (Emeritus), Western Seminary, Portland, Oregon

With well-crafted words, vivid imagery, and poignant scenes, Marilyn Weisenburg tells the heartbreaking story of losing her son David. At times, her honest narrative made me weep. But it also made me realize that there is something—maybe only one thing—stronger than grief: the grip of God's divine grace that never lets us go.

**Sarah Thebarge**, author of *The Invisible Girls and Well*

There's nothing more painful than losing a child. And no magic answer makes it all better. But there is the power of sharing our stories. In *Empty Branch*, Marilyn Weisenburg powerfully chronicles her journey of lament, sharing the raw and honest brutality of processing her son's tragic death in Iraq. Her fierce prose walks unflinchingly through the valley of the shadow, taking a sledgehammer to the religious platitudes and Hallmark clichés that are often given to the grieving. Yet her journey does not land there, but travels through the trenches into the presence of a God who is big enough to take everything we've got to bring—and is present with us in our pain, to bring us not ultimately to an abstract "answer," so much as to bring us to Himself.

**Joshua Ryan Butler**, Pastor at Imago Dei Community (Portland, Oregon)
Author of *The Pursuing God* and *The Skeletons in God's Closet*

FINDING HOPE
THROUGH LAMENT

# Empty Branch

A Memoir

MARILYN WEISENBURG

Bonnie,)
His grace is
singing over
you.
Much love,)
Marilyn

Published in the United States by Credo House Publishers, a division of
Credo Communications, LLC, Grand Rapids, Michigan
www.credohousepublishers.com

ISBN: 978-1-625860-79-8

Cover and interior design by Frank Gutbrod
Editing by Donna Huisjen
Cover image by Shutterstock

*Printed in the United States of America*
First edition

In loving memory of our precious son,
David James Robert Weisenburg
May 2, 1978 – September 13, 2004
Always in our hearts.

For my husband, Jim
Our children and their spouses:
Elizabeth and Erik Railton, Jason and
Cindy Weisenburg, Daniel and Adina Weisenburg.
And for our grandchildren:
Aubie, Lincoln, Elliott, Silas, and Quinnleigh.
Beloved, courageous family, together on the journey.

# Contents

# Prologue

Mount Scott lies southeast of downtown Portland, rising above the Willamette Valley about 1,091 feet. Willamette National Cemetery is on the northeast side of Mount Scott. From the slopes of Mount Scott Portland sits to the west and to the east, with amazing views of the Cascade mountain range. From higher points on the east side of the cemetery, one can see the majestic Mount Hood. On a clear day, from the freeway driving south, if I look up to the left I catch sight of the American flag from the arena at the top of the cemetery.

When our oldest son, David, was in the Boy Scouts, he would join the throngs of local scout troops to place flags on each grave to ready the cemetery for Memorial Day weekend. This was quite an undertaking, its being the largest national cemetery west of the Mississippi. He was proud of doing his part to prepare for all the visitors and ceremonies that would take place over the long weekend in May.

We now live just five minutes from the cemetery. We often hear the military flyovers of F-15s as they break the news that another veteran has been laid to rest.

Our friends Rick and Jeanne live on the opposite side of Mount Scott, closer to Willamette National Cemetery. Jeanne told me once that on Memorial Day weekend she hears taps being played. I imagined the mournful melody reaching outside the grounds and wafting throughout the nearby neighborhoods. Jeanne shared that when she hears taps being played she thinks of us and of our son David.

That sacred ground at the cemetery is a place I've become accustomed to visiting after the death of our firstborn son in Iraq. Sometimes I visit David's grave alone. At other times my husband, Jim, joins me. Friends have joined me a few times over the years, too, as has our family.

There are times when I see another mother, or perhaps a grandmother or friend, laying fresh flowers on the grave of their loved one. Our eyes meet. We speak of our children.

I have wept with these grieving mothers and grandmothers when we've met on this holy hill. We've told each other our stories. As we listen intently to one another, we once again honor the one who has given their best, their life. We honor one another by the telling and the listening.

Sometimes we stand side-by-side, subdued and quiet. Words need not be said. There is a lament on our lips as we mourn together for our children who have died before us. It is a privilege to hear the broken stories and weep with those who weep. It is a privilege to be ushered into a place to which few invitations are offered.

In the past, when I thought about what life might look like for my adult children, it was outside the realm of the possibility that Elizabeth, Jason, and Daniel would mark the passing of one of their number. I never pictured them standing on the sacred grounds of Willamette National Cemetery, laying fresh flowers on their sibling's grave. I only imagined college, travel, careers, marriage, . . . and, someday, grandchildren. When an adult child flies away to war in a foreign land, the possibilities of different stories emerge, however, and we live with the tension and fear of harm. It was certainly unfathomable to me that we might bury a son.

I recall a biblical story of two sisters in the town of Bethany in Judea, mourning the death of their brother. I remember reading about their confusion and sorrow. When Jesus arrived and saw one of the sisters weeping, He was deeply moved in spirit and troubled, and He wept. When Jesus saw Mary weeping, He broke down and wept alongside her.

When I visit my son's grave and weep on the sacred hill in Portland, I know that I'm not alone. I know that the One who wept with Mary weeps with me.

# Chapter 1

# September 13, 2004

The newer model white SUV drove with caution up the forested hill toward our home. My husband, Jim, drove behind them and wondered whether the afternoon sunlight was obscuring the driver's view as he searched for an address. The tentative driver seemed unfamiliar with our tucked away neighborhood. There was only one way in and out. A sign near the entrance announced "Dead End."

Jim turned into our driveway and parked the car. Following the long day at work, his eyes landed inadvertently, as they so often did, on the yellow ribbon tied securely around the large old oak tree in our front yard, and he let out a deep sigh. He turned and began chatting with a neighbor, Bob, who had stopped by to share some of the crisp, homegrown carrots he was hauling back from his garden with another neighbor's horse.

As they conversed, both petting the horse, the SUV that had driven slowly past our home made its way down our own driveway. The sun hit the windshield in such a way that Jim was unable to see the faces of the two men now parking. Our garage blocked the glaring sunlight, and

Jim was able then to clearly see the two soldiers in dress uniform. His eyes met those of the drivers, and suddenly my 6' 3" husband was bent over, gasping for breath, asking over and over again, incredulous, "Has my son been killed?"

Both soldiers immediately jumped out of the car and made their way to Jim's side. The driver asked, "Are you Mr. Weisenburg?" to which Jim repeatedly responded, "Has my son been killed?" before finally acknowledging, "Yes, I am Jim Weisenburg." They would not answer Jim's question until Jim had identified himself. The other soldier asked, "Is your wife home, Mr. Weisenburg?" He answered mechanically, "Yes, my wife is home."

In the living room I was talking to a friend, trying to work through my hurt and bewilderment in a phone conversation after learning the week before that my position at the church for which I worked was being eliminated. I was blindsided by the job loss and puzzled about how I would navigate the next four months working alongside the very men who had decided to phase me out. I was sad and heartbroken. I loved my job working with the young people at our church.

Hearing voices, I turned left toward the back door that leads to the garage. As I caught a glimpse of who was walking through, I said a quick goodbye to the friend I had phoned earlier.

I still cannot recall whom it was I was talking with. Was that particular memory loss trauma induced?

*Who was she?*

*What did she remember about that day?*

*How did I end the conversation?*

*Did I hang up on her?*

*Why does it matter?*

Jim walked in, but he wasn't alone. The expression on my husband's face was one I had never before seen in our thirty years of marriage; he seemed terror-stricken, and his eyes were full of panic.

It was then that I saw the two soldiers in their dress uniforms, following Jim with somber faces.

My eyes met Jim's, and we both knew the outcome before they opened their mouths to speak. We knew military protocol; there were no illusions about what their presence might mean for us. I stepped quickly to Jim's side. Major Hagadorn introduced himself and the chaplain who accompanied him. Then he spoke those cruel words of death, inserting our son's name into the telling. He spoke softly, but clearly, with tears streaming down his face, "The Secretary of the Army regrets to inform you that your son, David, was killed in action."

As he spoke the words it felt to both of us as though a heavy weight had crashed down through the ceiling and landed on our backs. Unable to stand and bear the news, we both collapsed on the carpeted floor, gasping for air. The devastating weight of a child's death was unbearable.

It was as though shards of a shattered glass ceiling were swirling through the air and hitting the floor around Jim and myself. Broken—all was broken. Broken hopes, broken dreams, broken hearts, broken lives, broken family, broken son. Everything around us exploded when those words were spoken. Would the destructive dust ever settle?

I remember screaming "*No! No! No!*" I don't recall how long the screaming lasted, hardly aware that the sound was erupting from my own mouth.

The heavy weight of the major's words kept me face down; I was screaming and clawing at the floor, as though I were searching for a cavern in the carpet into which I could crawl and hide. Confusion set in—*David was here in August . . . Did I hold him and kiss him goodbye one last time? How could David be dead?*

It seemed as though all the colors of this world had been bleached away, as though life's ongoing musical accompaniment had screeched to an eerie halt.

Jim was able to make his way to a chair and sit down, and the officers sat across from him. My legs wouldn't carry me; it seemed I was unable to pull away from gravity's clutch. As I finally crawled toward the couch, the chaplain began to speak. His words were carefully chosen and articulated as he described our son's final moments: "David was outside the wire, patrolling the roads near of Camp Taji, north of Baghdad. He was in a convoy of four Humvees. David was sitting behind the driver, in the second vehicle. They came under enemy attack, and there was a firefight. Suddenly an IED was detonated under David's vehicle. David died immediately." He promised that we would receive a more detailed account the next day.

I remember feeling sympathetic toward these men, assigned to this duty of delivering the worst news parents could ever receive. I saw the pain etched on their anxious faces. I remember that I wanted to say comforting words to them, to somehow ease their sorrow, but I was unequipped to hold their pain in conjunction with my own.

My first question was "How was David killed?" Major Hagadorn's previous words and explanation were simply not registering. He gave the account again, softly and respectfully.

My second was "Did he suffer?"

He repeated, "David died immediately."

Jim remembers that I asked these same questions repeatedly. I couldn't wrap my head around what we had just been told.

For several years this scene would replay over and over again in my mind, relentlessly haunting me as though delivering again and again the jolt of the horrific news these men had been assigned to deliver.

Day and night.

Night and day.

Haunting me.

Hissing at me.

They walked into our home with their drawn faces and steady, quiet voices on September 13, 2004, at 5:30 p.m.—immediate precursor to the moment they told us our son had been killed in Iraq.

It had been only two weeks earlier, in late August, that we walked with David into Portland International Airport for his six a.m. flight back to Iraq—back to the war zone.

We were unaware, when he checked in that morning, wearing an army uniform, that we would be allowed to walk to the gate with him if we were to acquire a special pass.

Walking to the security area and seeing that there was no line, we sat down for a few moments to say our goodbyes, holding him and praying with him. After a while we slowly walked over to get in line at the security entrance, after which we accompanied him to the first checkpoint, still with no line in sight. The security agent looked at us and back at David and asked whether we were his parents; there is a definite family resemblance, so I'm sure she could tell. When we responded in the affirmative, she asked whether we had a pass to go with him to the gate in Terminal C. Surprised that we could have attained such a pass, we sadly answered "no," whereupon she looked at us kindly and said, "Go ahead and go through with him, since there's no line!" She may have looked at our driver's licenses—I don't remember. What I do remember is being ecstatic that we could walk to the gate with him.

We stopped at Starbucks and bought him anything he wanted. *Anything at all—you name it, David, It's yours.* He settled for very little—coffee and a piece of fruit. We slowly walked to the gate together, David, Jim, and I. We wanted these moments together with our son to last as long as they possibly could. We didn't have to speak; we only wanted to be with him. And then it was time.

Time for David to depart and fly away.

There have been too many of these goodbyes with our two military sons. One of our younger twin sons, Jason, was in Iraq with the Marines for nine straight months. We didn't have to say goodbye to him a second time or send him back to the war zone simply because he had no leave time during his deployment.

Passengers were starting to board the plane, and we listened for his group to be called. David was one of the last to board, and he walked away after our final hugs. Once his ticket had been checked for the last time, he turned his 6' 4" frame back toward us, smiling his beautiful smile. He tried to make it easier for us, in our agony. He waved goodbye, and we watched him turn and continue walking. My tall, handsome son with the deep brown eyes.

And now they were telling us that he wasn't coming home, that he wouldn't be returning!?

We stood at the airport that day helpless and alone. I wanted to scream and tell them to stop the plane from taking off. I wanted to do something to prevent it from leaving the gate. Who in this world sends their son back to war after he has spent time in the safety of home?

I felt hot tears filling my eyes and spilling down as we began to walk away. The implications of what we had just done overwhelmed Jim, as well, so much so that as we walked down the long terminal he fell to the floor and wept. At that point neither of us cared who witnessed our tears. We had just put our son on a plane headed back to war. Everything in us screamed *No!* I had not birthed my babies to send them off to fight in a military conflict so far from home and safety! I was the mom who didn't allow her children even to play with toy guns.

We didn't say the words, though we shared a strong premonition that our son would not be returning to us. We'd had fears when Jason left for his deployment for Iraq, as well. Jason had been part of the Marines first expeditionary march into Baghdad at the beginning of the conflict in 2003. There had been so many unknowns at the beginning of the war. Chemical warfare was in the forefront of our minds, and the very prospect was terribly worrisome. It was difficult to sleep at night as we thought about our son at war.

When David left after his deployment with the Oregon National Guard, we both had the sense that he would not be returning to us. It seemed as though we were holding our breath for nearly two years, during both of our sons' deployments in Iraq.

I was kneeling next to Jim as he wept on the airport floor. After a few minutes passed I took his arm in mine and we stood together before walking out of Terminal C and leaving the airport.

It was a gift of grace that David had been allowed to come home for his sister's August 14 wedding that summer.

Only four weeks earlier we had celebrated the wedding of our only daughter and eldest child, Elizabeth. And a beautiful wedding it had been, in an idyllic setting at the childhood home of her husband-to-be, Erik, on the Oregon Coast. The Railtons' home sits high above the ocean and commands a most stunning view from Arch Cape north to Cannon Beach. The wedding was held in their beautifully landscaped yard.

Elizabeth, Erik, and his parents had worked hard to prepare the surroundings for the wedding. It was clear that day, neither too warm nor overly chilly. It was a small, intimate ceremony with only family and close friends in attendance.

The rehearsal took place on the afternoon of August 13, 2004, at the Railtons' home. Our son Jason and his wife, Cindy, planned to pick up David from the airport in Portland and drive immediately to Cannon Beach for the rehearsal dinner.

It was a gift of grace that David was able to leave Iraq at all that week in August. He had just phoned us on the previous Sunday to report that his leave had been cancelled due to accelerated activity, meaning that any travel out of the country had been put on hold. After days of our hoping that the travel ban would be lifted, David's commander had indeed given him permission to carry on with his plans. David was able to make the trip toward Kuwait and wait for military transport in Kuwait City before proceeding on to Oregon for his sister's wedding. His commander had made a blanket declaration that no one would be taking leave, and yet this man himself had made an allowance for David's trip home. We often speak of the Lord's kindness in bringing David home to celebrate with us and our family. We learned years later that a fellow soldier had implored the commander to make allowances for David's leave.

I was concerned about this abrupt transition from a hot war zone with the 1st Cavalry to a peaceful, ocean side wedding. I wanted to keep from badgering him with questions about his experiences, opting instead to thoroughly enjoy his presence with us as we celebrated Elizabeth's special day.

Jim and I, our son Daniel, and his fiancée, Adina, arrived at Doogers Restaurant in Cannon Beach for the rehearsal dinner. There was high anticipation in the air that David would be arriving soon with Jason and Cindy. We stood on the corner with Daniel and Adina waiting for Elizabeth as well.

It was 5:30 p.m. on August 13, 2004.

We spied Elizabeth's car moving toward us from the south end of South Hemlock, at almost the same moment turning and spotting Jason's appearing from the north, on Hemlock. The two cars met directly at the intersection and turned simultaneously onto Sunset Blvd. Yes, they turned at the same moment, the drivers playfully enacting what appeared to be an abrupt swerve to avoid a head-on crash between them and then they were maneuvering as close to one another as they possibly could. Elizabeth's eyes were dancing with joy when she caught sight of her brother David on the passenger side of Jason's car. The enormous grin on David's face at the realization that he had made it home for his sister's wedding made my heart leap with excitement as I observed from my corner vantage point. Recollection of the joy dance of Elizabeth and her three brothers, as we entered the restaurant, was a gift Jim and I continue to cherish.

Moments later Elizabeth snapped a photo of David and me sitting together, my mama heart full of joy. This picture, unbeknownst to us, would be the one displayed in newspapers a month later and painted or sketched on two separate occasions by artists we had never met.

Though exhausted from his long flights from Iraq to Oregon, David seemed fully engaged on Elizabeth's wedding day. I remember seeing the tears in his eyes as his sister glided arm in arm with Jim toward her groom. David and Elizabeth were the best of friends, and he was grateful to be sitting with his family, grateful to witness his sister's marriage to Erik Railton. It was a beautiful, brief, meaningful ceremony, with Elizabeth and Erik complementing each other well. We all agreed that the two were well matched and were delighted to welcome Erik into our family.

The rest of the day was suffused with delight—a memory to be treasured for the rest of our lives. A beautiful, joyful day, surrounded by friends and family.

Sadly, this most delightful day of vows, dancing, and celebration will forever be associated in our minds with the darker aftermath so soon to follow. Little did any of us realize that this was to be the last day our family would be together, whole. The deep ache that remains within my daughter over that cruel juxtaposition, that association of fulfillment with finality, is a sorrow I lament as well.

David spent the next two weeks of his leave with us in our new craftsman style home, built adjacent to a par-three golf course. We had moved in only a month before the wedding, and he had immediately fallen in love with our home and its peaceful setting. We are grateful to recall his brief stay with us here. David, as well as Daniel and his fiancé, Adina, traveled directly to the wedding from the airport. None of them had been able to tour our new home, to which they drove together after the wedding, until that happy time.

When David and Daniel entered our home for the first time together, Daniel remarked that it just didn't feel like home. David, looking around with an appreciative laugh, responded, "Are you kidding? It has Mom written all over it!" I smile wryly whenever I recall his words. David knew me well. Our hearts were knit closely together.

Those two weeks whirled by in a blur. David visited Elizabeth and Erik often after they had returned from their honeymoon. He also visited friends in Portland, and we held an open house at our place, both for David and for the newly engaged Daniel and Adina. Soon afterward Daniel and Adina flew back to Omaha to begin another year at the University of Nebraska.

David looked at condos in downtown Portland, hoping to purchase a home for himself after his deployment. He wanted a place in close proximity both to his work in the office at Star Park (a position being held for him) and to Portland State, where he was planning to finish his degree. He loved the idea of living downtown.

The evening before his return to Iraq we enjoyed a family dinner. David was late. This was a common pattern of his, and Jason seemed irritated. At last our son made his appearance, bearing a dozen peach-colored roses for his mama. Winking at Elizabeth, he quietly quipped, "You know I'm her favorite, and now I just scored big time points!" Jason rolled his eyes and announced, "Let's eat!"

It was nearly unbearable to face the reality that we would so soon be dispatching this young man back to the battlefield in Iraq. I tried to make light of the inevitable, to make my serious son grin and laugh with me. I looked up at this tall young handsome man and said half seriously, "David, you don't have to go back! You can go AWOL!" His response was startling; in hindsight I should have expected it. He gazed at me with earnest eyes before replying, "Mom! I have to get back to my men. They need me, and I need to be there." I was struck by his loyalty, courage, and resolve for the mission at hand. His strong conviction of the need to take care of his men and to do his job to the best of his ability was admirable. I was also struck by the reality of the physical pain he was enduring for the sake of his mission and men. He would barely speak of the serious back pain he endured, minimizing his own discomfort for the sake of the greater good.

David had written to his sister, a nurse, asking her for suggestions to alleviate the throbbing pain, of which we hadn't been aware until Elizabeth had informed us. He had a slight curvature of the spine, something he had only learned in his adult years, the scoliosis having gone undiagnosed when he was younger.

During his leave he made an appointment with a private doctor, not wanting the Army/National Guard to be aware of his medical issues in light of the possibility he might not be allowed by return to Iraq after his leave. The doctor did indeed determine that David's back issue was serious enough to warrant release from his deployment.

Rejecting this assessment, David insisted that he would return to his men and mission in Iraq. He asked for medication for pain management, to which the doctor reluctantly agreed, David gamely insisting that with the medication he would be able to endure the pain until the end of his deployment in March. It was only after his death that I realized that David, based on his serious medical issues, would not have needed to follow my half-serious request to go AWOL.

And so, two weeks after the wedding, at four a.m., Jim and I drove our son back to Portland International Airport.

It was two weeks later, on Monday, September 13, at 5:30 in the afternoon that the two uniformed soldiers entered our home with their chilling, horrific communication. Our oldest son had been killed while out in a convoy of Humvees, patrolling the roads north of Baghdad in Taji,

Iraq. There had been a firefight and an IED, and he had, mercifully, been killed instantly, along with the driver of the Humvee, Ben Isenberg. There had been three others in the Humvee, two of whom were injured. The incident had taken place after 4:30 p.m. Iraqi time on September 13.

The two soldiers entered our home exactly one month after David's arrival in Cannon Beach for Elizabeth and Erik's rehearsal dinner. I sat there stunned and horrified, the shock of their message and its import leaving me breathless, speechless, and benumbed.

In that moment our lives were changed forever.

# Chapter 2

# Phone Calls

Initially when Jason deployed, and again when David deployed, Jim and I had independently rehearsed whom we would call first in just such a crisis as this. Without telling each other, we had both thought seriously about the possibility of having to make those seemingly impossible calls. We couldn't bring ourselves to discuss the matter even to each other, and neither of us ever mentioned that we had formulated a plan. Voicing the unspeakable aloud was a burden we each chose not to impose on the other.

They began to arrive shortly after our initial calls—our first responders and dear friends. We were desperate for their presence as we proceeded to contact our other children. Jim's first call was to our longtime friends Barry and Denise. He then phoned our friends and neighbors Gregg and Renee. I called Clark and Cathy, with both of whom I had worked in youth ministry.

Before our friends arrived Jim and I talked through the necessary calls to our daughter and twin sons. We looked at each other helplessly, with disbelief in our eyes. The very idea of telling them about David sickened us. We longed for another story, not this one.

*Please, dear God, not this one!*

At the moment we were groaning over the calls to our children, our twins, Jason and Daniel, called us from separate locations on our respective cell phones. We spoke with reservation as we talked briefly with each of them.

As I responded to Daniel I told myself, "This is craziness, carrying on a brief conversation knowing I just heard David has been killed." All I could bring myself to say to Daniel, after asking him whether he would be available and whether he was with Adina, was that Dad or I would call him right back. Jim said the same thing to Jason. They both said yes, we could return their calls. We knew we needed to gather ourselves and prepare for the conversations. I don't believe either one of them suspected anything was wrong at the time. When we finished those short initial conversations we numbly shook our heads at each other. "How can we possibly tell them?" *Couldn't we just float away?* My sorrow was for my husband and my kids; I was at this early juncture numb to my own pain. I would have preferred to do anything else than call them back and inform them that their brother wouldn't be coming home.

Elizabeth lived here in Portland; Jason was stationed in Southern California, at Camp Pendleton; and Daniel was living in Omaha. I despised the distance between us and our sons at this critical time.

As Jim and I gathered our thoughts we talked about our hope for each of our kids to be with someone when we called with the news about David. I yearned to be physically present with each one of them, to comfort them with my embrace.

At about this time Clark arrived, his face pale and drawn. He sat with us as we decided which of our kids to phone first. When all three of our boys were in high school, Clark had been their youth pastor. Now all three, as adults, were his friends. Clark was very quiet, his head bowed as Jim picked up the phone to make the calls. He shared vicariously in the dread we felt as Jim dialed the first number.

Just as Jim was about to call Daniel, my phone rang and I answered to the voice of my friend Jody. She was in Lake Tahoe, vacationing with her husband, Dan. Jody and I prayed regularly together on Monday mornings, her son serving alongside David with the Oregon National Guard in Iraq. Thinking it was out of character for her to make a call while away with her husband, I answered quickly, but all I could get out was her name. Realizing immediately that something was terribly wrong, she waited as I haltingly spoke the words announcing David's death. I asked her to pray for us as we were about to make the phone calls to our children and remember hearing her saying *"Oh no! Oh no! Dan, no, no!"* as we ended the call.

I can't begin to imagine the horror that must have slammed this unsuspecting friend in the face. Being that closely tied with us and having her own son, Caleb, in

David's unit, she must have waited in agony for her son's phone call, longing to hear his voice once again.

Jim wanted to call my cousin Gary before reaching out to Daniel. Daniel had lived with Gary and his family for a couple of years while attending school in Nebraska. Gary, a pastor, is not only a very kind and compassionate man but a safe and trusted friend. Gary and Laurie were on their way out of town when Jim called. After speaking with Jim and hearing his horrific news, they immediately turned around and headed back to Omaha, back to Daniel.

Barry and Denise arrived, red-eyed, before we made the call to Daniel. We couples had attended the same high school in our teen years and had raised our children together. David and their son, Graham, had been buddies since childhood. Later, Graham would speak about their friendship at David's memorial service, and Barry would deliver the eulogy. It pained Barry deeply to have to consider doing this for his best friend's son.

The pain of our son's death was deeply etched on their faces as they walked through our door. With intensity, Barry embraced Jim and began to weep.

Denise held my face tenderly in her hands and gazed into my eyes with such searching. It was as though she were imploring me to please, please tell her this wasn't true. I could visibly observe at that point the truth sinking in, and she too was overcome with sorrow.

I didn't understand why so few tears were in my own eyes and wondered vaguely why I felt so dry and empty, as though I could simply drift away. I felt like a shell of a person, hollow, and in utter disbelief.

At the same time, however, the gravitational tug of the floor held me in its powerful grip. I didn't know I was in shock. I certainly didn't know that the shock would last for a very long time.

When Jim made the call to Daniel, he spoke with Adina first. Adina handed the phone to Daniel, and Jim spoke softly: "Buddy, I'm so sorry to tell you this horrible news about your brother . . ." After Jim explained what had happened to David, we could hear this son's excruciating wails. I cannot find the words to express how helpless we felt, unable as we were to reach out and hold him. The shattered pieces of my heart broke into yet smaller shards as Daniel wept. I heard Clark whisper in consternation, "This, this is too intimate for me to be here . . ."

Clark was our close friend, and we trusted him implicitly. How could we express to him that we sorely needed the strength and courage his presence brought us?

When Daniel's cries subsided he was able to briefly discuss with Jim his plans to fly home immediately. Knowing as we did that Adina would be an unfailing support to Daniel, we were grateful that she was at his side, that he wasn't alone. We were grateful as well to know that Gary and Laurie would be with Daniel soon.

Renee and Gregg, our friends who lived across the street, had by this point arrived. I had never before witnessed such pain on their faces. While I felt as though

I were walking slowly through a dream, looking into their very real faces helped the reality of David's passing to slowly begin to sink in. *Oh God, please, please, can this just be a bad dream?!* Their faces told me otherwise. And Renee's tears etched the reality into my consciousness.

I was thankful that Renee and Gregg were present, grateful that they lived just across the street, profoundly appreciative of their unquestioning willingness to dive so deeply into our lives and our home from the moment they heard about David's death. Together they cared for all the details of running our home for what seemed to be weeks, taking turns, along with others, to answer the ever-ringing phone. They organized the running of our home for the next few weeks while we were too numb to think about our own needs.

I was grateful for Gregg and Renee in the following months, for all the times they would drop by for visits, asking us at appropriate points in our conversations to tell them stories about David. Since we were still new neighbors, they had met our son personally only once, when he was here on leave. They wanted now to know him better. Did they have the slightest inkling how beautiful it was for them to come alongside us, to decline to attempt to rush our grief? Did they begin to recognize how beautiful a gift it was for them to speak our son's name and ask us to share his stories?

The last of the first responders arrived: Clark's wife, Cathy. She raced in, breathless after rushing to our side after attending to her own kids, who were also deeply shaken by the news. David had been like an uncle to them, and they loved him. When Cathy saw the rest of us, I witnessed reality visibly slapping her in the face. Her entire mien and body language changed, and I saw grief overtake her. She looked as though she might collapse on the floor. I wanted to go to her, to try to comfort her. But I myself couldn't yet rise from that magnetized floor.

We began to agonize about calling our son Jason. He was a Marine, based in Southern California near Camp Pendleton. His roommate was a Marine as well, but not having his number we found ourselves obliged to call Jason without the benefit of his having a friend at his side. It made me nauseous to think that Jason was alone, without family around him. Though he was married to Cindy, she lived near us here in Portland. They flew back and forth to see each other often, and soon he would be living in Portland with her.

We quietly talked with our friends, who agonized with us, realizing that we couldn't put off the inevitable any longer, that Jason needed to know. We somehow had the presence of mind to recognize that if we were to call the Red Cross first this step would expedite Jason's leave for home; I was profoundly grateful that this son could return on so short a notice.

I worried about Jason, already a veteran of war at the age twenty-three. Having been with the first expeditionary unit that had marched into Baghdad in 2003, he had already experienced the war in Iraq, less than a year before David had arrived. Jason knew the sights, the sounds, and the smells of war, and I worried that those sensuous memories would haunt him. I worried about the What ifs? including whether PTSD might overtake and get the best of this vulnerable young veteran of war's atrocities?

Jim called the Red Cross and spoke with them briefly before calling Jason, following through by immediately phoning our son before the Red Cross could get through to him. Jim wanted to ensure that it was not a stranger who gave his son the news. Again, the over-the-phone sound of a son's wailing was horrendous.

Finally, Jim called our daughter, Elizabeth. He first called the cell number of our son-in-law, who cheerfully answered the phone. We could hear his tone change as he took in the news Jim was conveying to him. He promised to proceed home immediately to be present alongside Elizabeth so she wouldn't have to hear the news alone.

Elizabeth was seventeen months older than David. They had always been very close and had communicated well, often without relying on the need for words. For the most part they had implicitly understood each other and been able to convey the hard things to one another. They had leaned on each other and confided in one another during some tough years when they were both in middle school. She had planned her wedding around the time of his scheduled two-week leave to ensure that he could be there to witness her vows.

It was almost too much to bear, now, to relate to the new bride this horrific news. My heart ached for her, envisioning how the news of David's passing might impact her life. I was overwhelmed thinking about how her newly wedded bliss might come to an abrupt halt, robbing her to some degree of the fresh joy she held with Erik.

When Jim spoke with Elizabeth on the phone her response was almost too much to bear. Her cries of disbelief and horror gripped my heart. I wanted all of this to stop immediately. *Please, dear God, please tell me this is a mistake!*

The excruciating sounds of pain and loss I heard from all of my children that day tore a gash in my heart. Death, that mortal enemy, in its ultimate cruelty ravaged our family, threatening complete destruction. I couldn't protect my remaining children from the pain and suffering of their brother's violent death. My lungs felt as though they were held in a vice grip, and I had to remind myself to breathe.

Outside our door the warm summer evening whispered the end of a lovely September day. Inside the ambience couldn't have been more opposite; we were enveloped by trouble, disoriented by confusion and disbelief. I was stunned to the core, my thoughts numbed to the degree that nothing made sense.

More faces entered. Friends from church. Should I greet them? I couldn't move. I couldn't breathe.

After a while someone announced to me, "Elizabeth and Erik are here now," and at that point I broke free from the grip of gravity the floor had held on me and rushed out to meet them.

I was overwrought with anguish for my husband and my children; facing my own pain was at this early juncture untenable—that pain was at any rate mercifully unreachable and wholly unattainable. I held Elizabeth in my arms; she too was in shock. She tried to speak but needed privacy, so we made our way, bereft mother and daughter, into our bedroom, where we stared at each other in disbelief, neither uttering a word.

A mother yearns in all trying situations to shield and protect her children. But a mother also opens her hands in a gesture of letting go, making room for those children to grow and stretch their wings, to fall down and get back up on their own. A mother spends countless hours on her knees, praying as they prepare to leave the nest. She wants her children to know as they flap those tentative wings, and more so as they take wing and fly away, that they are loved. A mother also acknowledges her inability to shield and protect them completely, if at all; we humans, no matter how well intentioned, lack the power to control life's sometimes cruel trajectory. But this! This was simply too much! Death threatened to cut us to the core.

I was restless and agitated not to have Jason and Daniel at my side as well. I needed to be near them, to see their faces, to hold my still animate and vital sons. A part of me would remain missing until they arrived.

This horror of war abruptly displaced my family. It was too painful to wrap my head around. As I held Elizabeth my anger—the first intense emotion I was able to strongly feel— began to simmer. I was stunned by my fierce reaction over the propensity of war and violence to rip apart families and mark each member with a repulsive wound, deep and agonizing.

Two days later I waited impatiently for Daniel to arrive from the airport. Adina's parents had made flight arrangements for him after he was too distraught to formulate a plan of his own. Adina would follow on a later flight. I was standing in the kitchen when Daniel walked through the door. He had been holding back his tears long enough, and the dam burst into helpless wails as I held him close. I was utterly at a loss to comfort my son, and this incapacity horrified me. My strong, six-foot three-inch son was completely broken.

Jason was on a flight home from Southern California on the following day. Jim and Daniel met him at the Portland airport, and Jim told me that when Jason spotted his twin brother he rushed through the crowd like a bull until he reached him. They held each other with a grim intensity, aghast at the horror of having lost their older brother to the violence of war.

When Jason arrived home I was sitting on the porch swing, away from the frenetic activity inside my home. I heard his distinct footsteps on the deck and knew it was him before he rounded the corner. When I saw his face I crumbled. Jason sat down next to me on the swing and held me close, fresh tears filling our eyes. I held him tenderly and tenaciously, with a mother's fierce love, never again wanting him to leave my sight. I didn't want any of my children outside my immediate purview ever again. Frantic thoughts about Jason and another deployment played havoc with my mind. What could I do to prevent that from happening? I was terrified to face the reality that Jason might indeed have to leave us again. I wanted to do whatever I could to comfort and care for my family.

On September 13 I figuratively joined a legion of mothers aching to comfort their children when deep, excruciating loss comes home.

# Laughter

David was a quiet man, . . . except when he laughed. When his friends would describe him, they invariably mentioned his laugh. When David laughed the windows seemed to shake. He laughed loud and hard. Especially when he got a Yahtzee.

A soldier friend mentioned that he could hear David's laughter from across the huge mess hall at Camp Taji, and he would know David was sitting somewhere inside the building, eating with his friends. It is good for this mama's heart to know that her son laughed at some points during his deployment to Iraq.

Pragmatic and practical, he entered the Army as a chaplain's assistant right out of high school, choosing the armed forces because we was unsure about what he wanted to study in college and preferring not to waste a moment of his life. Beyond his sense of humor he was a serious young man who felt it would be a waste of time to go to school without having a solid goal in mind. When he left the Army after four years, he had planned to attend Portland State University to study criminal justice and psychology. At the same time he registered for school, he signed up for the Oregon National Guard.

That description of David—someone who didn't want to waste a moment—seemed to be a part of his DNA. He was born ten days before his due date, on May 2, 1978. As a child he often ran ahead of us or whomever else he was with at the time . . . much to the chagrin of his grandparents. He was organized, thrifty, and practical, which is part of the reason he embraced the Boy Scouts so readily.

David was organized already as a young boy preparing for Boy Scout camp, and there was no reason for me to come alongside and help him. He had it all together. He would write a list of everything he needed for the trip and draw boxes next to each item. He then taped his list to his suitcase or bag. As he packed each item he would make a checkmark in the appropriate box. Funny boy.

I maintained a list like that for camping with our family, and he may have watched me in action as I packed every item necessary for a weekend away. I needed to stay organized for my own peace of mind. We were alike in many ways, David and I.

David was also a sensitive, gentle, tender soul, who cared deeply for his friends and family. And he loved extravagant gift giving. When he was only a little guy he already relished selecting just the right Christmas gift for every family member, carefully thinking through his list and what each person might like to receive. He never had to be reminded or prodded along. At Clark Elementary

School in Portland he couldn't wait to shop with the money he had saved for "Santa's Secret Workshop" and took pleasure in selecting gifts for his loved ones. When he was in the Army, stationed at Christmastime in Seoul, Korea, he was granted leave for the holidays and arrived home bearing gifts for the entire family. Beautiful gifts, each telling a story about the Korean culture. He bought me a beautiful, blue silk robe with "Mommy" monogrammed on it.

He loved to tease his sister, who was seventeen months his senior. While learning to walk, clinging to the edges of the coffee table, he picked his way as quickly as he could toward her, growling deeply and relishing her shrieks. We nicknamed him "Bear."

His joy in hounding and harassing his sister continued into their adult years. Once, as she was showering and steaming up the bathroom mirror, David and Daniel, wanting to play a prank on her, went a little overboard in their attempts to traumatize their older sister.

Daniel crept in and wrote on the mirror "I know what you did last summer," while David slid all the kitchen knives under the door, strategically placing mops and brooms outside it. Yes, she shrieked once she stepped out of the shower . . . the exact response and sound they were expecting to hear.

We remember his humor and his thoughtful ways, as well as his sarcasm and cynicism. We remember when he wrestled with his faith and carried heavy burdens.

Not being a verbal processor, he tended to internalize his struggles, distancing himself from loved ones for a time and worrying that he would suffer rejection. At such times we were aware he was struggling and prayed for protection and grace as he worked through whatever may have been on his heart. We asked the Lord for insight regarding our quiet son, and I worried incessantly, not only about him but about all of the circumstances I couldn't control. Having two sons deployed to a war zone had to a large extent cured me of any absurd notion that I could control anything in their adult lives, but that didn't mean I hadn't been tempted to worry or attempt to orchestrate events since then. It only implied that I recognized much more readily than before the futility of such magical thinking.

One reality David clearly understood when he went to train for battle in Iraq was that he was loved. We never skimped on expressing our love, and he readily received it, knowing at all times that no matter what, he was our son whom we loved very much.

When David was in high school, he was proud when his older sister entered nursing school at Azusa Pacific University. He was proud of the scholarships she received, as well as of her goal of becoming a nurse and her drive to finish well. Practical and thrifty from a young age, he was also troubled and concerned about the alarming amount of debt she was incurring. We were reminded of David's values and fiscal planning in a visit with Herb Hammerlynck several days following David's death.´

Herb, the Casualty Assistance Officer assigned to our family, gathered us for a meeting once we were all together for David's memorial service. We asked Cathy to sit in on this meeting to take notes and ask questions we might forget or be too numb to consider. Her capable presence, both physically and mentally, was a comfort, relieving us of the need to strain to remember the details Herb communicated to us. Also joining us was Jon Moore, who was on leave from his own deployment in Iraq. Jon, a longtime friend of both Jason and Daniel, was in David's unit, and it was his mother, Rhonda, who prayed with me on Mondays. Jon felt like family to us, and we wanted him near. Of course, Cindy, Erik, and Adina joined us as well.

Herb asked our kids whether they had any questions about David's death. I believe I spaced out to the degree that if they did ask anything (and I vaguely recall that they did) I don't recall the details. I do remember viewing this as a painful, unusual way for our family to meet; the atmosphere felt suffocating, and there was an almost palpable tension in the air. We enjoyed being together as family—but not like this.

To gather together without David in our midst felt counterintuitive and wrong. We searched one another's faces with unasked questions in our eyes, some logical and others inadvertent, a step removed from the reality we all knew. *Where is he? Is he late again? How can we be together without him? How will we navigate this? How will we function? Will we ever laugh together again? Will we always feel this raw? Will the joy of being together always be overshadowed by grief and pain?*

Being together, but not *all* together, was devastating, leaving the sensation that a part of ourselves and our identity had been unceremoniously ripped away. Each of us was left with a raw, oozing wound, feeling empty and angry.

Herb talked to us about when we could expect David's body to arrive and who would be his military escort. We all understood, ultimately, that he was with us on this miserable day to help plan David's memorial service.

First Herb began to speak about David's life insurance policies. I kept my eyes down for the most part; it seemed like such an effort to lift them. Once again gravity pulled. It pained me to look up at the faces of my children and observe the unmasked sorrow in their eyes. Their drawn expressions broke my heart. It seemed absurd—an outrage, almost—for a family to discuss a life insurance policy at a time like this! *This is backward. This isn't right. It's all out of order.* It would have seemed more reasonable had the topic been one of their parents' policies, not their brother's. The situation felt crass.

I kept seeing, in my mind's eye, those two soldiers walking into our home, and I wanted to scream while there was still time to reverse the inevitable, "Go back, go back out; go away and don't speak!!! *GET OUT!*" The hypothetical picture of such rejected reality played over and over again in my mind, uninvited but inexorable. I tried to stay focused, but the seemingly magnetized floor and the irreversible temptation to check out vied for my attention and energy.

Herb cleared his throat and launched into a discussion of the life insurance policy from the US Army. It was, according to David's specific instructions, to be given entirely to his sister, Elizabeth. He had always been worried about her college debt. Although she had graduated from nursing school nearly seven years earlier, he still fussed over her, to the extent of making provision for her, in the case of his death, to pay off her student loans. We sat stunned, all of us, shocked by a gift so loving, generous, insightful, and practical. Elizabeth looked at each of us with questioning eyes; I suspected she may have been worried about her younger brothers' reactions. Months later, after she had paid off her loans, she did in fact divide up the balance with the two of them. David had always been a planner, but I didn't expect that he would plan with this kind of unselfish insight and practicality.

Herb then told us about David's high school buddy and fellow National Guardsman, Peter Helzer, and his request to act as military escort to David. Peter was to fly from Dover to Portland as David made his final trip home. This was a comfort to us, knowing that our son would be with a dear friend and fellow soldier like Peter. We had known Peter for more than ten years, the two young men having become friends during their freshman year at Benson High School, where they were both on the swim team and had both played saxophone in the school band. We were honored by Peter's gift of accompanying David home. There would also be a soldier who would fly from Iraq to Kuwait, and another from Kuwait to Dover Air Force Base in Maryland. Never would David be alone on his final earthly flight.

While our son's body was in Dover, the news of an absolutely unexpected provision of love and respect overwhelmed us with gratitude. As processing took place in Dover, a chaplain was with David throughout the entire process—present from the moment his body arrived to the moment he departed, with Peter, bound for Portland. The chaplain later wrote to us the most kind and loving letter, explaining his presence there as a witness during this sacred time. He relayed to us how David's body had been painstakingly identified and prepared for its journey home. His words exemplified the high degree of respect and honor conferred upon our David at this time.

It wasn't coincidental that this chaplain connected to us, he being the husband of a friend of mine. The manner in which this came about was a story only the God of comfort and the Father of mercies could have penned. My friend Jody called our mutual friend Daryl, who lived on the east coast, to tell her of David's death. Daryl's husband, Jason, a chaplain with the Air Force, was at the time based near Dover. Aware that David's remains would be flown to Dover, Jason asked permission to function as the chaplain on duty for the entire processing after the arrival of David's body, and this was granted. David's remains arrived with a military escort from Kuwait, and from the time of its arrival through the night until Peter's arrival from Portland, Chaplain Jason Knudeson watched over our son. He was present for hours, without breaks and without sharing the responsibility with anyone else. In his letter he wrote with tenderness as he described his watching over our son—his sacred duty and honor, born from love. The letter itself, as well as his personal presence, brought us a God-breathed comfort and an unexpected assurance. This kind and godly man described not only an honoring but a holy and sacred passage.

Since then Jason Knudeson has served in the Air Force all over the world. At this time and in this place, in 2004, he was strategically on hand in Dover, and in our minds and hearts we were convinced that he had been placed there by the hand of God.

We continued on in our meeting with Herb and began to map out the memorial service, which was ours to plan and prepare for. We decided that the event would be held near our home at New Hope Community Church, a facility large enough for the number of people expected. Our own church would not have accommodated such a crowd. Following the memorial service would be a graveside service at Willamette National Cemetery in Portland; the military would make the arrangements for this aspect.

We wished to maintain our privacy to the degree we were able, not wanting the media and their cameras at either service. They particularly needed to keep their distance at the graveside service; we simply couldn't fathom having cameras in our faces or questions being asked of us or of our family and friends.

As a family we talked through what we thought David would have liked at his service. He loved jazz, having been in a jazz band and playing his saxophone in high school, so we asked a friend, a jazz pianist, to play soft jazz during the prelude. He readily agreed.

The question arose of who would speak at the service. Jim, Elizabeth, Jason, and Daniel all wanted to share. Our friend, Barry, would read the eulogy, and Clark would offer a brief message. In addition there would be a slide-show presentation of David's life, and my cousin Gary would close the service in prayer.

Wanting a deeper, heartfelt and personal description of David's life, spoken by both friends and co-workers, we invited some of his friends, from childhood to the present, to share some stories about David and their relationship with him. Everyone we invited agreed; even though a few were less than comfortable with public speaking, their love for David won out.

Our planning took an awkward turn when Herb pointed out that it was customary for the governor of Oregon to speak at the memorial services of fallen soldiers from our state. Governor Kulongoski had spoken at several services to date, but it seemed overwhelming for us as a private family to come to grips with how public that aspect of the service would be. We are also known for our strong opinions.

We agreed that this was not a venue for making political statements or offering convenient sound bytes for public officials. Then Elizabeth asked the down-to-earth question, "Well, did Ted know David?" Our son's friends and co-workers had indeed known him and would share personal stories. The air was thick with tension, none of us wanting to compromise on this one. Herb was surprised, though he honored our wishes to opt out of the governor's message at the service.

As it turned out, even though Governor Ted Kulongoski didn't speak at David's service, he took it upon himself to make a personal connection with each member of our family, a heartfelt gesture endearing him to all of us. He had our respect, and we knew we could count on his support.

Later in the evening, when the planning was finished, several of David's closest friends came to visit. They gathered on the deck, which overlooked a par-three golf course called Eagle Landing. I gave them space as they hung out with our kids, along with their spouses and fiancée. All of them were close to us, like family. Some had attended the same schools, and all of them had been members of the same church youth group in high school. Each had spent many evenings in our home throughout the years.

One friend, noticing that no one was on the course golfing at the time, grabbed one of Jim's clubs and started hitting some balls onto the course. Soon everyone was grabbing clubs and hitting balls, striking them as hard and arcing them as far as they could. A contest ensued. Who could hit a ball farthest, into the wooded area beyond the greens? Hearing the commotion, I came outside to watch.

Looking back, I think I was laughing and crying at the same time—not to mention a little worried that the manager of the course might notice and point out the rules. *David would have loved this*, I acknowledged, adding to myself, *He should be here.* I could almost hear his laughter.

After a little while this hitting of golf balls evolved into something more serious than a contest, taking on a solemnity of its own to the point that it seemed almost ritual and significant. The growing intensity of these young men spoke volumes about the depth of their hurt, confusion, and grief. All were in their mid-twenties, just starting out in life and making young men's plans for future studies, travel, marriage, starting families, or purchasing their first homes. War and the death of a friend and brother had certainly not been a part of the equation for any of them. But here stood these intruders, smack in their faces, and they knew instinctively that their presence was wrong— foreign to their thought and expectation patterns, surreal and unimaginable.

David's friends had continued to love him, even though he had been distant the past few years from at least a few of them while studying at Portland State. They had a long history together, and he would always be one of them. Now he was gone, and this reality didn't seem to compute. In reaction these sensitive young men hit those golf balls as hard and as far as they could, until they were exhausted. There wasn't much they could say about their newfound sorrow; they would have to work through their grief, each in his own way. I wished I could ease their sadness, but I was at this point still numb to my own grief, unable to do anything beyond holding them each tightly and loving them. I had few words, but I unapologetically shared their tears.

For years now this group has continued to meet on David's birthday, in the evening, just to be together and remember their friend. They endear themselves to me every year when they gather to share a beer and remember. As they meet I wonder whether they can hear the sound of his laughter, as it used to be when they were young, in the same way I do.

Since David's death most of his friends have married and started families of their own. I follow their lives on Instagram and Facebook and occasionally see them at birthday parties and weddings and at church functions. Elizabeth remains close with several of them and their wives. My heart aches for my son's absence in their lives. This is a deep and unresolved pain; I have few words to describe it. *What is this still tender tension grabbing at my heart? Is it jealousy marking my tears? Why do I at times struggle so with seeing their lives go on without him? Perhaps it's the anger and the reminder of the robbery death is.*

Three of David's friends from his youth group were in his graduating class, though David was the first of the foursome to leave home and fly away after graduation. Before he left a tradition was born in our home. The four graduates met here and plopped down on our couch together, asking for a picture to be taken.

This ritual of gathering in our home, on our couch, would continue for several years, whenever they were all in Portland at the same time. They would plop down on the couch and strike the same pose, and an image would be snapped of their reunion. It was fun to see these teenagers mature into young men, beginning to sport facial hair and becoming adults. They were like brothers, good friends. I miss those carefree times, the rushed gatherings to snap the photo before any one of them was obliged to run out the door, drive to the airport, and fly away.

Death has robbed us all of David's inclusion at the gatherings and the photo ops. When I view their pictures or hear their stories, I wonder what might have been. If David were still among them, of what would the ongoing sagas consist? Perhaps that's it. I'm missing the stories and the vibrancy of these vital young lives walking through my front door.

And my son's infectious laughter . . .

## Chapter 4

# The Final Trip Home

Our CAO, Herb Hammerlynck, was unsure of the exact time and date of David's final trip home. This was dependent upon military transport from Dover to Portland, though it was a high priority. We waited for the day anxiously, as the rest of our plans for his service were dependent on his arrival in Portland.

Jim and I spoke about the day David's remains were to be returned to us. It was an abbreviated conversation, the subject being one I could hardly bear to speak of. I was completely undone thinking about it and found it hard to comprehend that this would actually be happening. This physical reality would render David's s horrific death more real than I felt prepared to accept.

I don't remember Herb talking to me about going to the airport to meet David's casket; perhaps I blocked out these arrangements. Angry about this war and with my resentment seeping into my reasoning about this major homecoming ceremony, I resisted the prospect of being in attendance when my son's decimated remains arrived in a casket draped with an American flag. In retrospect, I wish with all my heart that I hadn't missed this homecoming. Before I beat myself up yet again over this lapse on my part, however, I hasten to add that I don't recall hearing from Herb or any other military official about the significance of my being present when David came home. All I remember was that we as a family were sickened to think of meeting a casket carrying David's body. I was too frozen to lean into the importance of being a witness to his final trip home. Still today I carry this as one of the deepest regrets in my life.

So Jim went alone.

I waited at home for him; I had not, in fact, left our house since David's passing more than a week earlier. Several of the pastors and their wives from our church who had wanted to come and pray were with us in our living room, as were Dan and Jody Mayhew. Our daughter-in-law, Cindy, was there, as were the others from our family, some with me and some in other areas of the house. We stared blankly at each other until Jody suggested that we pray. Cindy's tears were flowing by that point, and I was still dazed with shock, dry-eyed and seemingly weighted to the floor.

As we were praying that evening, Jim was driving north on I-205 in our black Explorer, bound for Portland International Airport. He didn't ask anyone to accompany him, nor did anyone volunteer. To this day it saddens me to think about Jim making this lonely, painful trip to the airport without support.

Jim had been instructed to turn right after the sign for the Delta Flight Center, which was close to the main airport terminal. He parked the car in the back of the building and was making his way toward the entrance when he saw Lt. Peter Helzer dressed in his class A uniform. When their eyes met Pete said simply "I'm so sorry!" and the two embraced. After handing Jim the cross David had carried on his person when he was killed, Pete led him around the corner and into the huge cargo bay through a doorway. There waited a hearse in the middle of the enormous building with David's flag-draped coffin inside. Jim also noticed six Portland policemen standing discreetly in a corner of the building.

Jim climbed into the back of the hearse and rested his hand on David's coffin. Opening his mouth to pray, however, he found that he couldn't utter a sound. He doesn't remember how long he sat in the back of the long black hearse containing a coffin with the remains of our son. What he does recall is feeling as though his insides were being pulled—no, forcibly yanked—outside of him. He remembers Pete being close by, ready to assist him if needed. At some point someone asked whether he was ready, to which he replied in the affirmative. Jim retraced his steps to our car and climbed inside alone, after which someone opened the enormous cargo bay door and they drove out, Jim joining the entourage outside the cargo bay. There would be a procession from Portland International Airport onto I-205 south and on up to Lincoln Memorial Cemetery, across the street from Willamette National Cemetery where David would be buried. The six policemen guarded the procession on motorcycles as the hearse and Jim made their way toward the freeway entrance. Jim reported later that the police were continually changing positions, though it seemed that there were always four in front and two in back. As with any other funeral procession, traffic was stopped so the vehicles could continue on unimpeded to their destination. By this time the twilit skies had given way to full darkness.

Upon arrival at Lincoln Memorial Jim was greeted kindly by the funeral director. Herb was there too, to be with Jim as the ceremony was completed. Each policeman solemnly and respectfully shook Jim's hand before discreetly retreating into the background. Jim spoke briefly with Herb before departing for home. He was shaking, devastated all over again, when he climbed into the Explorer. He drove around Mount Scott toward our home, full of friends and family awaiting his return.

All eyes were riveted on Jim when he re-entered our home. Jim has a strong presence about him, and heads seem almost inadvertently to turn when he enters a room. My husband has a distinctive, serious face, not to mention that he stands more than a commanding 6' 3" tall. Making his way over to me, he understatedly announced, "Here's the cross David had in his pocket when he was killed," placing it in my open palm. I realized with a start that I was touching the last gift I had given David before his departure for war.

This was a necklace with a silver cross he had initially given to me one Christmas when he was a young boy. I had worn it often, but when he was deployed to Iraq I had re-gifted it to him. I felt utterly undone as the story unfolded in my mind. I looked up at the friends surrounding me—Vicki Abbate, Joan Browning, Cathy, Jody, and their husbands—and tearfully filled them in about the history of the necklace. I remember Vicki's eyes brimming with tears. I wanted never again to allow that necklace out of my grasp. It was one of the last items David had touched, a vital, physical connection to him.

I wished already that I had felt strong enough to have gone with Jim; *We should have been there together* was the convicting message replaying over and over again in my head. My feet still felt magnetized to the floor at home; the inexorable weight that had crashed through the ceiling at the news of David's death continued to hold me in its vice grip.

A day later I would finally leave the house with my family and proceed to Lincoln Memorial for the viewing. We negotiated the winding road from the southwest side of Mount Scott to the northeast side and through the entrance to Lincoln Memorial. Directly across the road from the entrance was one of the side entrances to Willamette National Cemetery, where David would later be buried. It is a beautifully forested area, over a thousand feet high and overlooking Portland, which is to the northwest of the two cemeteries.

Together we walked into the funeral home, Clark and Cathy accompanying the eight of us. Inside and to the left were blue upholstered benches set against a wall of windows with the morning sunlight shining though. To the right of the long, wide hallway were a few rooms with doors closed, between which was one with its doors wide open. It looked like a chapel, and soft, serene music suffused the space from overhead. David's cousins Paul and Sarah sat on the bench directly in front of the viewing room with the doors open. The funeral director, whom Jim had met the night before, led us into the viewing room and invited us to stay as long as we wanted.

Slowly and almost awkwardly we filed in and sat near the front on the left-hand side. I heard others walking in behind us and noticed that Jim's sisters from Missouri and Southern Oregon had joined Paul and Sarah.

As a collective family unit we sat in stunned silence as we contemplated the flag-draped coffin containing our David's remains. It was surreal to reflect that he was in our midst, though not truly present. I was in a state of denial and disbelief, feeling agitated and somehow still convinced that this was not happening. *Why are we here? What are we doing? I can't accept his death as reality!* I wanted to leave, run—get the hell out of there. When I couldn't hold myself together any longer, I mumbled to Jim that I needed to leave. I felt suffocated, unable to wrap my head around the fact that this coffin lying before us held David—or what remained of him—within it. I couldn't fathom the reality that he was no longer living and breathing. Desiring to run from Lincoln Memorial as far and as fast as I possibly could, I actually stumbled out slowly, as though in a dream. Jim walked out with me, along with Clark and Cathy. I believe that the kids stayed behind and spoke with Jim's sisters, but I didn't feel up to making conversation with anyone. I wanted only one thing—to get out of there.

It was to be an inordinately long day, beginning with the closed casket viewing and followed later by David's memorial service at New Hope Church, a large church that sits above I-205 near Sunnyside Road, on the southwest side of Mount Scott less than a mile from our home. Its doors are frequently opened for large public funeral services, as well as for college graduations. Stephens Road lies in front of the church, and at the main entrance is a traffic-regulating roundabout. To the west of the roundabout one can enter the New Hope parking lot, while to the east lies Eagles Landing, an eighteen hole, par-three golf course overlooked by several condos, town homes, and single dwellings. Our home borders the north side of this course.

In the center of the immaculately landscaped roundabout stands a flagpole and a monument called "Guardian Spirit," installed earlier in 2004 by Rip Caswell Sculptures. A bronze eagle, wings outstretched, perches high atop a large boulder a bit south of the flagpole—a beautiful sight as one drives through our neighborhood. The flag in the roundabout was flying at half-staff. In fact, on Governor Kulongoski's order, all flags in Oregon were to fly at half-staff on September 21, 2004, the day we buried David.

Portland, Oregon, was the city David had loved with a passion and for which he had interned while in high school. In addition, our son as a teen had worked as a lifeguard for its community pools. At the time he was deployed David worked as Assistant Operations Manager for Barry Schlesinger at Star Park in downtown Portland, living in downtown Portland, near his work and near Portland State University, where he was a student. To think that all of the flags in Portland were being flown at half-staff in honor of David on this sacred day seemed a stunning tribute. To know that people beyond the scope of his friends, family, and military family were thinking of him, and of us, made me feel as though the entire city was encircling and watching over us. I marveled at how the city David had loved so deeply was now loving and honoring him in return.

As Jim and I drove into the parking lot at New Hope Church, I was taken aback by the Patriot Guard Riders, dressed in leather and lining the long driveway, each holding high the American flag. The sight, in fact, nearly took my breath away. These individuals were there out of respect and to counter the horrendous actions of the representatives of Westboro Baptist Church of Kansas who were there to *celebrate* a military death, insisting that this was God's punishment on America for tolerating homosexuality. The kind actions of the Patriot Guard Riders kept our gaze from falling on the protestors, and for that I remain deeply grateful. Since that day, each time I attend another military funeral or memorial service I am overcome with tears, profoundly appreciative for the presence of this noteworthy and remarkable group of men and women, the Patriot Guard Riders. No grieving family members should be met with the callous hatred and insensitivity of the Westboro Baptist Church protestors and their disgusting signs.

David's cousin Adam, who had traveled from Nebraska for his service, is close in age to our two younger sons and is one of the most respectful and kind young men I've ever known. Raised in a military family, this young man was attuned to our every need on this day. He rode with Jim and me to the service, and when I realized I had forgotten something at our nearby home Adam offered to drive over and pick it up for me right away. He was there and back so quickly I hardly noticed his absence. I suspect that if I had voiced the need for a different pair of shoes for the service he would have driven to the mall, picked one out for me, and been back before I could blink my eyes. He was that attentive.

We were instructed by a military official who greeted us after we drove past the Patriot Guard Riders to enter the church through a private entrance on the south side. An official, Sergeant Herzog, would escort us into the building and into a large room behind the pulpit area, our family members accompanying us as we walked into the meeting room. This official would be the point person overseeing both the memorial and the graveside services, his duty to act as a personal guard over our family. He was solemn and serious about his duties, and I'll never forget his watchful eyes. It seemed as though whenever I looked up Sergeant Herzog was at my side, ready to care for any need throughout the entire day.

As our family gathered in the back room we noticed high-ranking military officers and their spouses discreetly standing by, waiting to greet us and offer condolences. The representative of the 1st Cavalry, 101st Airborne, and 3rd ID was in attendance from Fort Benning, Georgia, along with every senior ranking officer in the Oregon National Guard, each of whom spoke with us and all of whom were kind and, it seemed, genuinely moved with sorrow over our loss. The officer who made the deepest impression on me was Major General Rees of the Oregon National Guard, along with his wife. I could see on their faces how saddened they were for us, and they spoke briefly and kindly. I have no doubt it was evident to them that we were feeling more than a bit overwhelmed. The chaplain who had come to our home on the day David was killed would be the main speaker at the graveside service.

We observed more people entering the back room from the left side. A group was nearing, and a military official introduced us to a man and his wife, both tall and solemn, who warmly embraced each of us after we learned that they were Ben Isenberg's parents. Ben's wife, Rachel, was there, as well. All of my pent-up and conflicted emotions seemed to collide against one another as we met Ben's family, with whom we sensed an instant bond brought about by our mutual loss: our sons had died in war together.

At that point I spotted someone peering through the crowd surrounding us—whom I immediately identified as Lt. Peter Wood. Peter had attended high school with our daughter, and he and David had afterward been deployed together. David had in fact reported directly to Peter while in Iraq, and Peter had been in the Humvee with David and Ben when it had been hit with the IED. Peter had been treated at Fort Hood, Texas, for some injuries received during the attack. We had requested his presence for David's service, if that were possible, and here he was. I embraced Peter, so thankful to see him alive. I have no idea what memories he lives with now. After we spoke briefly with Peter, our next visitor arrived and wanted to meet the entire family. We were standing in a receiving line meeting all of the people in attendance, including Governor Ted Kulongoski and his wife. An aide walking with them personally introduced each member of our family to him.

I hadn't expected to meet the governor of Oregon on this day. All of the fanfare was new to me and to our family. Governor Kulongoski had a personal greeting for each of us and even seemed to know in advance a little about each one of us. He conversed with Jim about how they had both grown up in Missouri and shared a personal story about his childhood. He spoke to Jason, dressed in his dress blues Marine uniform, about their shared experiences as Marines, and shook Cindy's hand, handing her a military coin—a significant gesture of honor in the military world. Cindy has carried that coin in her purse for the past nine years. He went on to speak with Daniel and Adina about school in Nebraska and finally with Elizabeth and Erik about her job as a nurse.

The governor seemed to go above and beyond the necessary in expressing to us his sorrow over David's passing. Although he wouldn't be speaking at our son's service, he stayed for the entire two-and-a-half hour service and then joined us for the graveside service as well. Several times Jim and I observed tears in his eyes. We understand that he has attended every service for a fallen soldier from Oregon, speaking at nearly all of them. We felt supported and buoyed up on this day by both the governor and his wife, and it was an honor to meet him.

It was time to make our way into the sanctuary for the service to begin. As we walked past Sergeant Herzog I was taken aback to see that the auditorium was filled nearly to capacity, with almost 900 people in attendance. To our left, in the audience, was a large section of military officials in their dress uniforms. Later on I learned that several parents and spouses of fallen soldiers were present as well.

A front pew had been reserved for us, and I felt panic welling up within me on the realization that it would not seat all eight of us. I tried to remember to breathe. *We need to all be together and this got overlooked?!* We squeezed together, managing to fit six of us on the pew. Daniel and Adina sat directly behind us, along with my sister Julie and her family. Frantic in my insistence that Daniel had to be with us, I felt as though I would come unglued. I was a wreck, knowing there was nothing I could do about this glitch that seemed so significant to me. Reaching behind me, I grasped Daniel's hand and held it for much of the service. I wanted him to be connected and needed from my side to be connected to him. I desperately wanted all of my children close by.

Clark began the service with prayer, after which Barry, Jim's dearest friend, read the eulogy. Then, one by one, the people from David's life whom we had invited to speak began their stories of knowing David. First up with his childhood friend Graham Capps, Barry and Denise's son, followed by John Bachman, his high school and youth group buddy. I had been concerned that John might be a little shy to address so large a crowd, but once he got going—recalling some funny stories about camping with David—he visibly began to relax. Two Benson High classmates, Lt. Peter Helzer and Lianne Brakke-Pound, took their turns, after which David's buddy Smokey (the only name for him I've ever known), a Portland DJ, took the podium.

David's Star Park employer and friend Barry Schlesinger was one of the final speakers. He surprised us by announcing a scholarship in David's name to Portland State University. His own sons, who had worked with David, were already drafting a brochure. Later on the Schlesinger family would honor David and his scholarship by committing all of the funds they would otherwise have spent on a downtown Christmas party to additionally fund the scholarship at PSU. David, always concerned about the cost of higher education, would have been immensely proud; now there would be funding for military personnel at the downtown institution he attended, Portland State University, through the David Weisenburg Memorial Scholarship.

After David's friends had spoken, Elizabeth, Jason, and Daniel took their turns, in that order. I can barely recall their words, though I remember them courageously standing there in front of hundreds of people. They all disliked public speaking but were more than willing to pay audible tribute to their brother. Daniel was the last to speak, and as he began Jason placed his large hand on his twin brother's shoulder to steady him, Elizabeth standing to her younger brother's right. I was proud of all three as they allowed their love for their brother to take precedence over their uneasiness regarding public speaking.

Finally, Jim spoke about our oldest son, referring to David's courage and readiness as a warrior/soldier to protect those in harm's way, as well as his strong sense of justice. As he spoke, a picture was displayed of David in uniform in front of a tank, holding a rifle. Jim spoke of David's gentle side, depicting for the crowd this one who had never been too busy to pause in small villages and engage young Iraqi children in play. The one who had asked his mom to gather school supplies for these children and mail them ASAP. And the one who, despite temperatures of 120 degrees or higher, and despite hefting pounds and pounds of armor and gear, would playfully throw the children into the air and catch them each time. A picture was shown of David doing just that in a village north of Baghdad. Jim juxtaposed the two sides of our David, describing our fallen son as a gentle warrior. This same picture of him tossing the Iraqi boy up in the air appears on the front of the brochure the Schlesingers designed for the PSU scholarship.

Clark too spoke briefly, after all of the other speakers were finished. He had some stories of his own to share about being David's youth pastor. One of the main points he wanted to get across was that David had known himself to be loved. His family, coworkers, and military family— all had loved him. What a beautiful story, Clark reflected; how extraordinary for one to be so highly regarded and yet, most of all, so loved.

My sister Julie and my friend Janet Himes had earlier in the week gathered family photos to be given to Patrick Ezell, who had prepared a poignant slide show presentation of David's life. The pictures appeared larger than life, projected there on the big screen at the church, and I felt enormously proud, not only of David but of my entire family. I felt at the same time as though I were in some kind of dream, viewing the parade of pictures of my own family along with those many others assembled there in that church.

Next came a military ceremony—something I had never before experienced. One by one officers stepped in front of the Fallen Soldier Memorial to the right of the podium. On a table, surrounded by lush floral arrangements, stood an inverted weapon upon which was perched a helmet. David's dog tags also hung from it, and his boots stood alongside. Two officers at a time stood solemnly in front of the memorial and then in perfect synch saluted, slowly walked toward the display, and placed a military coin upon it before turning around and making their way back to where they had been seated. I lost track of how many took part in this ceremony, in which Governor Kulongoski also participated. We were all deeply touched by the precision, the honoring, and the respect offered to our beloved David.

At the end of the service my cousin Gary graciously closed in prayer. We all wanted to personally inspect the memorial with the coins, so we stood and began to walk over. Just as we were about to reach the front of the table, however, one of our boys' childhood friends, Nathan Kleen, hurried to our side to give us hugs. He was joined almost immediately by another friend, Linda Kebbe. With tears coursing down her cheeks she embraced me, and as she did it seemed as though at least half of the audience surged forward to stand in line and offer their condolences. Going off script in beginning to greet our friends and family, I couldn't help but catch Sgt. Herzog's pained expression, but he would have to accept the course deviation. This wasn't going to be on precise military timing: our David had been a civilian soldier.

There were many who came forward to briefly speak with us. I was so touched by the group of elementary school teachers who wondered whether we remembered them. Of course I did! They had taught all four of our children at Clark School in southeastern Portland. We were astounded that they had come . . . as we were amazed by the presence of the throng of others we hadn't anticipated. It seemed surreal to see in one place all of these individuals whose lives David had touched in one way or another.

I don't recall at what point Sgt. Herzog caught our attention, but when he did it was to announce that it was time to proceed to the graveside service. It seemed as though we walked rather briskly out of the church before getting into our car to drive in the procession, which made its way around Mount Scott to Willamette National Cemetery.

Once at the cemetery Sgt. Herzog led us to some chairs set up for the family, after which we waited for the next ceremony to commence. This would be entirely a military ceremony, one with full honors. While our guests thronged the large shelter I glanced to one side and spotted our friends Peter and Blythe, before looking to the other side and catching sight of other friends, Kevin and Lori. We were surrounded by close friends and family, and I began in spite of the day's tension to relax a bit. This was a very quiet, solemn service. Standing near the front and to our left were high-ranking military officials, along with Governor Kulongonski and his wife.

As the ceremony was about to take place, the pallbearers walked in with the flag-draped coffin carrying our son's remains. I'll never forget the solemn, perfectly synchronized marching of Army soldiers acting as pallbearers. There was one Marine pallbearer at the right front, there in his dress blues Marine uniform: our son Jason, standing there looking resplendent, tall and proud in his 6' 4" frame, looking straight ahead. After the coffin was set down, the pallbearers turned toward one another and began to fold the flag.

Jason received the flag and then offered it to the governor, saluting him, before finally rejoining the family. He collapsed in tears as he sat down, never having expected to perform this honorary rite on behalf of for his older brother. My heart broke for both of my military sons as this younger one wept.

With tears in his eyes and the flag in his hands, Governor Kulongoski knelt down before me, humbly handing me the flag and, if my fogged memory serves me correctly, thanking me for my sacrifice. I can't imagine how he had made it through more than a hundred of these services. At one point during the day he shared with Jim that he was relieved to have been freed from speaking at David's service, taking each soldier's death as hard as he did.

A woman representing a group known as the Gold Star Moms at this point formally walked over to me, knelt, and spoke about my new status within this sisterhood, assuring me that the other Gold Star Moms would support me as I negotiated this journey of grief. She handed me my own Gold Star pin to wear—something I have proudly done at various military events and for other fallen servicemen.

The chaplain spoke briefly, after which we heard the flyover of helicopters. When David was in Iraq he had been a member of the quick reactionary force, which flies in on helicopters and is first on the scene, so helicopters were used for this flyover. Unaware of this arrangement, and thinking it very low to attempt to get a shot of the graveside service, when I heard the helicopters nearing I mumbled disgustedly to Jim, "Damn media!" Jim assured me that this was the scheduled flyover, not the media! I don't know why, but this story still makes me chuckle, and at this solemn moment my misconstruing the situation came as a cathartic instance of comic relief. Why in the heck did I suspect the media would actually work that hard to get a picture of my son's funeral? I realize now that I simply wasn't thinking clearly.

As quickly as it began the flyover was ending, and the twenty-one gun salute started up. It was a chilling sound, those sharp reports repeated over and over again in rapid succession. I felt each one from my insides, as though these military personnel were standing right next to me. I was shaken, as was the rest of our family.

Ending the brief ceremony came the lilting and lonely sound of Taps being played by a single soldier, up on a hill overlooking the shelter where we sat surrounded by friends and family. This was our cue that the service, dreaded and yet beautiful and memorable in its way, was over. When we stood up I felt so exhausted I wanted nothing more than to return to the car and be alone. I remember seeing a picture of ourselves walking out of the service with glazed eyes, obviously wooden and completely spent. I knew that I would see most of these people again at our home, where a meal was being prepared by Ruth Ann Richards and Christie McLean, so I didn't feel it necessary to greet more of them at this moment. Surely all would understand that we were emotionally wrung out.

We watched mutely as David's coffin was carried from the shelter and placed back into the hearse to make its way to his burial site. Unaccustomed as I was to military protocol, I didn't understand the reasoning, but it wasn't part of the plan for the family to be present for the actual burial. Days before the memorial service Herb, our CAO, had explained to us how this day was to proceed, concluding with an enigmatic "You aren't expected at the actual burial. They will do it later." There being no further explanation, we had simply nodded numbly in acknowledgment. It hadn't occurred to us at the time to ask whether we might be permitted to break protocol and witness the interment of our son.

Much later, however, this seeming omission—which had become a regret with which I felt a need to wrestle—became an issue to discuss with my grief counselor. I felt robbed of the closure of participation in this final step of bidding farewell to my son. I had most certainly been present at his birth, of course, and now, against my poignant desire, I wasn't so much as permitted to witness his being lowered into the ground. I struggled for a long while with head games playing out in my mind regarding his burial.

I was weary of these men of war—of their arrogance and the costliness of their decisions. I was weary, too, of the men at church and their seemingly arbitrary decision leading to the layoffs of three women. I was weary of these men who had deigned to make overriding decisions concerning the private burial of my own son. I was weary of thinking about all of this, longing only to retire to bed and shut down.

Back at home after the graveside service, many friends and extended family members joined us for a meal prepared by friends from church. The crowd poured out of our great room and onto our expansive deck. I felt loved, supported, and encouraged by the presence of these familiar supporters. Later that night, as I lay in bed exhausted and finally still, profound grief enveloped and overwhelmed me. At that moment I wanted only for the thrusting, intrusive thoughts in my head to turn off and let me be. I craved peace and at last allowed myself to cry out in lament to that One called the Prince of Peace. I trusted implicitly, despite the jumble of my emotions, that He was even at that moment talking to the Father about my pain.

What, even today, am I to do with the negative thoughts that still upon occasion plague me? I didn't and do not want an easy answer or religious cliché to somehow ease or even to erase my pain and solidify my trust in the Lord. It angers me when a person's deep sorrow is minimized and expected to be reduced by pat religious answers. These types of messages neither offer hope nor bring peace to a broken heart but only shame the hurting for failing to "have enough faith."

Throughout the following months, as I struggled with overwhelming grief, I was nonetheless suffused by a sense of an unusual grace in the midst of it all. The severe mercy in my struggle was in the struggle itself, and in the grace that abounded even in the midst of the wrestling. I was convinced throughout of an utter lack of shame and judgment from my Savior, who was instead pouring out upon me His grace and lovingkindness. I sensed a degree of peace only His holy Presence could have supplied, even within the tension and my continuing felt need to grapple those insistent questions and the meaning behind these heartaches. Grace was extended to me by the strong arm of my God, as though He were saying "*I know,* and *I AM* with you."

# Chapter 5

# Letters

It felt revolting to have to tell our children that their brother's Humvee had been hit by an IED while patrolling the streets of Baghdad, instantly killing him. Conveying this information was a horror in and of itself, yet we had been touched and traumatized by it, too. My thoughts were frenzied with concerns for my living children.

When one child has been taken out, the parent often worries that the others are vulnerable as well. Although I had no choice but to allow these young adults to fly away in the trajectories of their individual choices, I was rocked to the core by the reality that I still held onto them with clenched fists. I didn't literally expect one of them to be ripped away from us, yet with every casual goodbye I feared they might not come home.

David's death abruptly and cruelly changed my perspective, my reality—my everything.

We were marked by others, seemingly irrevocably, as parents who had lost a child. That became our identity, and we became a part of that exclusive club everyone else shudders at the prospect of joining.

I had, of course, been aware from the outset of David's responsibilities in Iraq. I had listened to his stories—though he had no doubt couched the reality in careful terms for my benefit—when he had been home on leave two weeks earlier. I also knew that being a part of the 1st Cavalry was a distinction carrying a dangerous weight in that particular time and place.

Now, despite my overriding peace, when I had a few moments to myself anger erupted within me.

*Why did my son join the National Guard?*

*Why did the leaders of war send the National Guard to Iraq?*

*Did those in the know plan for an extended stay in Iraq?*

*How many more casualties of the war would there be? Even one more would be too many!*

I already knew, of course, some of the answers regarding David's choices. He had believed he could make a difference. He had truly loved his country, his freedom, and his personal mission to serve with pride. I must admit, as a child of the tumultuous sixties and seventies, that I was a bit cynical in my thinking; no military influence in Iraq, I was convinced, would contribute to lasting change.

I was more than a little cynical about David's involvement in the war . . . until we began receiving the letters, until I began to learn more about my son's influence in that broken, war-torn corner of the world.

The letters poured in after David's death, day after day, week after week. Sometimes, after all these years, we still receive them. There have been letters written to comfort and encourage us. Letters from strangers across this country, from people we've never met. Letters from grateful Americans who kindly followed through on an impulse to thank us, to encourage and bless us. Letters addressed to us to convey vicarious sorrow on our behalf. Some have arrived with gifts, like handmade blankets and quilts, to honor the fallen and comfort those left behind.

Then there have been the letters from those who worked alongside our son, both in the Army and in the National Guard, as well as from those with whom he worked before and during his deployment in Iraq.

We have received letters from upper commanders who attest that they had never before known such a squared-away soldier as our son. Letters came from the soldiers alongside whom he had labored daily, telling us stories about our son we might otherwise never have known, because he had been too humble to share them with us—beautiful stories of a staff sergeant who had been deeply loved, respected, and honored. These individuals spoke of a *gentle warrior*, one in whose company they were proud to have served.

Gentle, because he had never been too busy to stop and talk or play with Iraqi children in the nearby villages they patrolled. He had cared and worried about those little ones. I remember his letters to us, relating the needs of these children for basic school supplies and encouraging us and others to supply the items on his list. We gathered and mailed school supplies for the soldiers to hand out to the Iraqi schoolchildren, for which David was grateful.

There were letters from childhood friends, from school friends, and from the girls on the swim team of St. Mary's High School. David, along with his own high school swim team friend Liane, had coached their team, Lianne as the head coach with David assisting her. David had loved the sport and thoroughly enjoyed coaching. Those girls made him crazy on the long bus rides back from swim meets, but he loved it. He acted like a grump sometimes, but inside he was smiling—though I'm not so sure how happy he was that time they picked him up and threw his fully clothed body into the pool, his cell phone still snug in his pocket. He may have been grumpy, I can't help but concede with a grin, as he climbed out of the pool—our tall and lean David, dripping wet in his street clothes. But he chuckled later on when he told us about it.

Those girls missed David. They wrote to us about him. They told us about a side of him we hadn't seen in quite the same way they had. They told us what an inspiring coach he had been, about how he had encouraged them to keep going as they swam in meets. I picture him running up and down the length of the pool, tirelessly applauding their efforts.

They invited us to their swim meets later on, during the season after his passing, and they presented us with a shadowbox full of pictures, mementos, and written thoughts about him. We were deeply touched by their gift. It was fun to personally meet these girls about whom David had spoken in endearing terms.

The letters we received were a testament to a servant leader, a gentle warrior. And they acknowledge, with respect, parents who have been marked by loss. The letters are a gift we keep carefully stored—treasures.

And so, in the midst of a country marked by protests regarding the war, my own perspective was changing. There were those who remembered that a family had buried a son, a brother, a friend. My heavy heart was kindly lifted, buoyed above the surface of the flood. I hadn't been expecting those beautifully written letters—or the love and respect they embodied.

*Mr. and Mrs. Weisenburg*
*Dear James and Marilyn,*

*I would like to introduce myself to you. I am the Executive Officer of Bravo Company (Bulldogs) 2/162.*

*My name is Nick G. Dordon, I knew your son David. I met David back at Ft Hood during the last week of December of 2003. David presented himself as a very mature man for being a young NCO (Non Commissioned Officer). He was the most energetic person that I have ever met. David was that person that I could count on to get things done and usually he had the items already done. It seemed he was always two steps ahead of me regarding the things I needed from him and his Platoon. He presented himself to everyone he met with respect and dignity. I personally thank you for raising such a professional, sincere, compassionate, Soldier, son and well-missed friend. And I thank you for having the chance of knowing such a man.*

*Myself and my wife send our sincere apologies to your family due to your loss of David. Enclosed are some pictures of David out on some patrol with my crew. I hope that these photos will help out.*

*Sincerely,*
*1st Lt Dordon, Nick*
*Fighting XO*
*Bravo co/Bulldogs*

I still wrestled with questions. The letters, though a comfort, could not in themselves sustain me. They could touch my heart, but only to a degree.

A wrestling journey yawned before me. It wasn't so much the *Why?* questions as it was those that sounded like "Where are You in the midst of war, job loss, physical pain—and now, in David's death? Where are You, God?" He seemed silent, if He was even close enough to hear. Yet on some level I knew in my head even in those early stages that He was present. I knew He had promised to be with His followers when we experience trouble—promised to be with us *at all times*. Then why did I feel so hollow? My heartache felt unbelievably deep and profound. I needed His touch of comfort, the heart sense to accompany the head knowledge that He truly was with me. Why did I feel so all alone and lost?

I tried to keep my feelings below the surface, to squelch those eruptions of angry thought. What good would my rage accomplish? Even as friends and family surrounded me, confusion enveloped me as well.

My anger was compounded by the budget cuts at our church, particularly when it came to the loss of my job. It still seemed unfair that I, along with two other women on staff, had been the ones to be laid off. What a can of worms an issue like this could open! When any thoughts about the job loss surfaced, I was upset and confused. *Why am I even concerned about my career at a time like this?* The guilt of those thoughts seeped in like poison.

In the night hours when everything was quiet, sleep eluded me. Nerve pain erupted—a chronic condition from which I had suffered for some time—searing hot, relentless. I wrestled with my thoughts, and quiet tears spilled onto my pillow. At night, when everything was still, reality refused to be squelched. I wouldn't hear my David's beloved voice again. I wouldn't see his endearing smile. I wouldn't grimace at his dry sense of humor or hear his louder than life laughter. I wouldn't touch his five o'clock shadow.

He had been torn away from us, never to return. How would we function as a family without him? How would we relate to each other? Our family dynamic changed dramatically when David died. Would we be able to relate to one another in the new rhythm our family was forced to accept?

Tears soaked my pillow. Sometimes Jim woke up when he heard my wracking sobs. We would go outside and sit on the swing together, holding one another close. When Daniel was still here he had a habit of coming outside to check on us. I sensed his worry over us. Sometimes he would sit with us, wordless in the silence of night.

Chronic pain was a constant companion. I experienced searing nerve pain in my arms, legs, and feet. In the first few days of hugs after David died, two friends sat on each side of me applying ice to my arms, which literally ached from hugging and holding loved ones, numbing the pain. Another friend massaged my feet. I appreciated their kindnesses to me, feeling that they were such true friends, sensing my needs and caring for me.

At night, when sleep eluded me, I grieved my compounded losses, which together seemed like robbery. I had, seemingly in one fell swoop, been robbed of my son, my health, my job. It was tempting to entertain thoughts about the diminished value I would have in the future. It felt as though my life were over. It all felt too big. It was too much.

This period became the dark night of my soul.

I felt as though the ground were crumbling and sinking around me. Mercifully, lyrics from the chorus of an old hymn—"On Christ, the solid rock, I stand, all other ground is sinking sand . . ."— played in a continuous loop in my mind. I was struck by the truth of Christ's being the only refuge and rock to which I could cling with certainty. At some point I would eventually fall asleep. Repeated nights like this led to a profound exhaustion.

I hated mornings. In the mornings I would wake up weeping. Reality would hit as soon as I opened my eyes. In the mornings my first jolting thought was that David wasn't coming home, and the tears would flow afresh. I didn't want to get up and face another day.

I wanted to talk to the Lord about all of this, yet when I opened my mouth to pray absolutely nothing came out. My heart resonated with the words of David, the lamenter in Psalm 69:

> "Do not let the floodwaters engulf me or the depths
> swallow me up or the pit close its mouth over me.
> Answer me, LORD, out of the goodness of your love;
> in your great mercy turn to me. Do not hide your
> face from your servant; answer me quickly, for I am
> in trouble. Come near and rescue me; redeem me
> because of my foes."
> (Psalm 69:15–18 NIV)

It has always my practice to seek the Lord in prayer—a part of my identity as a woman who seeks to know Christ and follow after Him. I love meeting with Him, meditating on His Word, and worshipping Him.

I met with other women to pray and study the Scriptures. Before David died I spent a week in Cannon Beach with other women in ministry, seeking the Lord corporately in prayer. This was a group of women from different churches all over the Pacific Northwest and beyond, who met with no agenda—just a time carved out from busy schedules to pray as the Holy Spirit led us. I prayed with the church staff and with the youth ministry staff. I prayed with students. I met with longtime friends to pray, too. I believe deeply in prayer. It is my lifeline to the Father.

I yearned to know the Lord and journey to the deep places with Him. I longed to go deeper with Him, both in prayer and in meditation on the Scriptures. I knew on an experiential level that I needed Him for every step and every breath. I wanted Him to lead me beside the cool waters and to restore my soul. I wanted Him to teach me more about Himself and His ways. I wanted to know how to love more deeply, to show kindness, to put others before myself. I wanted His wisdom as I navigated the world of chronic pain.

When David was killed I almost heard the door slam shut. I'm talking about that place of comfort and of the knowledge that Jesus was there, listening. THAT door. It was as though there were a huge steel door between the Lord and myself . . . that was threatening to slam shut, propelled by the winds of trouble. And so it was that when I opened my mouth to pray, absolutely nothing came out. The shock was so very deep. I felt myself to be adrift in a wide-open space; the really terrifying aspect was that I suspected my anchor was no longer attached to Him. I was floating away . . . *Did He know?*

I recalled King David's laments when he felt as though the Lord were not listening to him. He pled with Him for mercy. My heart resonated with the biblical David's during that season. No vocabulary was available for me to utter my heart cry, to articulate the convoluted jumble of thoughts and feelings that swirled within.

I was numb.

In shock.

Broken.

My anguish plummeted me to depths beyond my imagination; I was terrified by the thought that perhaps my God was deaf and mute when it came to my trouble. At night, in bed, I stared at the ceiling, pleading for mercy. I was about to take a journey that required me to trust the Lord implicitly through the darkest of hours. I did declare my trust in Him, but at the same time I was stunned to envision him turning from me in indifference, silent in my most desperate hour.

My lament over my own David had begun.

*"To You, L*ORD*, I call, You are my Rock, do not turn a deaf ear to me.*

*For if You remain silent, I will be like those who go down to the pit.*

*Hear my cry for mercy as I call to You for help, As I lift my hands toward Your Most Holy Place."*

*(Psalm 28:1–2)*

Throughout the first two weeks we had many visitors—our families and friends, the people who cared. People walked courageously into our home to be present and to weep and grieve with us. I was grateful for their presence. And yet I felt so alone, as though I had been translated to another, disconnected universe. They were there, with their families intact, . . . while I was marked. Different. The manner in which we would relate had changed.

When my sister Julie and my friend Janet worked together in the dining room to gather photos of David for the slideshow to be shown at the memorial service, I averted my eyes. I couldn't bear to look at his image. It was too much to take in the innocence on the face of my tender little boy.

Just two days prior to David's death I had been speaking with a friend at a youth conference in a large church near our home. Another friend was there, too, playing the guitar and leading worship. How absurd it was to so soon afterward be in the planning stages for our son's memorial service to be held at the same church! At the time I was wondering whether this conference would be the last youth event in which I would participate due to the impending loss of my job. Even though I had been given a timeline of four months before my termination date, I wasn't certain I could continue. It really didn't seem to matter any longer.

That evening, after talking with my friend at the conference, another friend and I drove to a birthday party together. We had both been invited to celebrate with a group of established friends, and we were the new ones added to the circle. On our way to the party we chatted about the implications of being included in this group. We laughed together before busting out into the old Dobie Gray song "I'm In with the In Crowd!"

Would I ever sing again? My heart was so heavy that the thought of doing so seemed far beyond my reach.

Would peace ever reign again in my heart, replacing the fear and dread I felt about the possibly of losing another child?

Would my husband and children make it as they worked through their own grief?

Would it be too much for them to bear?

Would I find myself in the comforting, merciful embrace of my heavenly Father?

Would I know deep down that even in this place of trouble, this place of doubt and uncertainty, He was truly with me?

Would I ever again be truly confident of His love and goodness? I knew in my head that His character never changed. But would experiential knowledge of permeate my heart and still me with His gentle peace?

Why was He seemingly silent in this dark night of my soul?

# Chapter 6

# Poem

Being the kind of mom who retained all of my gifts from the kids over the years, I searched our home now for anything and everything David had given me from his childhood on. Some were still in boxes since our move in July.

I was particularly driven to locate all of the personal things David had given me; they felt like a connection to him. I needed to touch those things David had touched, to imagine detecting a scent of him among the findings.

We tackled the bittersweet task of going through the boxes of his belongings mailed to us from Iraq, as well. The only item that hadn't been returned was a projector he had purchased before his deployment so that he and his men could enjoy some down time watching movies. We had instructed them to keep the projector; David would have wanted them his men to have it through the duration of their deployment, whereas it would only have sat here gathering dust.

We touched everything in the boxes that were sent to us—his clothing, his books, his Bible, and the leather journal I had given him to use during his deployment. We looked for those places he had marked in his Bible to determine what had brought him comfort and assurance. We felt strange and somehow vaguely guilty looking into his wallet. Jim took out everything and inspected each item, including Iraqi dollars displaying the image of Saddam Hussein. There was desert grit in the boxes mailed to us, precious dirt from the place he had last walked and worked and from which he had protected our freedoms.

We placed his belongings from Iraq in boxes in our garage and eventually emptied the boys' storage unit of everything that had belonged to David. We have an oversized garage, and the shelves were filling up with boxes belonging to him. David had kept everything from the time he was young—literally everything: binders full of schoolwork, notes, books, awards, mementos, pictures, music, movies, shoes . . . and more shoes, and clothes. Oh my word, did he have an array of clothes!

We found a thank-you note from Cathy, expressing her appreciation to him for helping with a move a few years before his deployment. We found notes written during Sunday school between himself and his friends. We found more notes from friends in high school. We found all of his Boy Scout paraphernalia and wondered together about his time with the Scouts. As a teenager he had been close to earning his Eagle Scout award, but as much as he had wanted this distinction he had also longed to buy his first car. So he had devoted the time and energy it would have taken to work for his Eagle Scout badge and chosen to work at Safeway instead. He'd had his eye on a '63 Chevy Malibu a friend was trying to sell, and after working for several months the Malibu, by arrangement, became his.

David was proud of his car and had worked hard for it, but I wondered whether he had ever regretted declining to wait a little longer for it so he could have experienced the distinction of being an Eagle Scout. For some reason I felt belatedly guilty about the matter, as though it had partly been my fault that he had opted for work over award. I don't remember encouraging him to stay with the Scouts another year or so. Had that been my fault? Why had he been driven to go to work as early as he could? Was all of this about the boy wanting his first car, or was the impetus something I had said or even implicitly expected? And why was I stressing about it *now*? Those regrets and wonderings must, I decided, have been a part of the processing of my grief.

I had a particularly vivid dream about David a few weeks after he died. I had hoped that I would see him in my dreams, and I did that night. I saw both David and Ben Isenberg, the young man who had been driving the Humvee when they had both been killed. In the dream David and Ben had each been driving a separate gigantic army vehicle, the kind used to clear land. They were in heaven, and in my dream they were clearing a flat, forested area to make room for their new homes, having chosen to live side by side. David looked at me with a huge grin on his face and waved. Suddenly he was standing next to me, smelling of hard work in the sun and wanting a cool drink. His arm around my shoulder, he was still grinning—excited to order sweet tea for refreshment. This sweet tea was even better than the kind with which he had fallen in love while living at Ft. Benning, Georgia, when he had been in the Army full time. He seemed so happy, so contented, so suffused with joy, with no trace of worry etched on his face.

When I woke up from the dream I tried to savor each element of it. I knew it was a gift to be treasured and wept with a deep longing to experience more than a single dream about him. I wanted to see him again, to feel his arm around me, to learn how to make sweet tea and offer it to him on a sweltering day.

One night after David's death, it was like he reached out to me. For several weeks after David had left to go back to Iraq, we heard what sounded like a phone alarm every night. We would wake up at 2:00 am to a beeping noise, but we couldn't find the source. We checked and double checked our cell phones and the beeping wasn't coming from either phones. After a short time, the beeping stopped and we went back to sleep. Weeks went by and one night at the designated time, the alarm woke us up. This time I was fully awake and on a mission to find the source of the nagging sound. I searched a drawer next to our bed and there it was, the PDA I used over the summer and thought I had lost. The annoying beep ended as I held it in my hand. Then a message popped up along with the 2:00 am alarm, it simply said, in bold letters: HELLO MOTHER. I was astonished,

David was the only one who called me Mother. I laughed at our prankster son, who apparently set this alarm when he was with us in August, then hid the device in our bedroom. I laughed and I cried grateful tears for this funny way he was communicating to me. He knew it would make me crazy; and I knew it was a way he was expressing his love to me.

Elizabeth and I went out to dinner together at Laurelwood, in the Hollywood district in Portland. We were talking about David when I told her about the dream, prompting her to share her own dream about her brother.

In her dream we were still living in our classic four-square-style home in the Rose City Park area of Portland. She was standing in the kitchen looking toward the dining room when she saw David standing in the corner, grinning at her. She exclaimed, "David! You're here! I've missed you! Where have you been?" to which he informed her that he was in heaven, exclaiming, "Liz, its wonderful here!" She said that his face was glowing and that she knew he was contented and so very happy.

We could barely refrain from sobbing, and yet we were happy to know we had both dreamed about him. *That we had both "seen" him and could confirm that he was happy!* No more back pain, emotional pain, war, or suffering. He was safe with Jesus. We were trembling—our pain, and yet somehow relief, too deep for words.

I continued to search our home for anything that had belonged to David, anything that hadn't already been packed up. I couldn't bring myself to look, however, at his childhood photos. Actually, I couldn't look at any of the childhood snapshots of our children. It was and still is painful to do so, knowing now, in hindsight, what was to be in our future as a family. I understand that this is common and even at the time understood that I wasn't going crazy.

As I searched I came across some of the pictures he had drawn for me as a little guy. I wept as I stared at those crude artistic renderings, so glad I had exercised the foresight to keep them! Before our move to our current home we had purged the unnecessary, downsizing in the way of empty nesters. But I hadn't been able to bring myself to let go of those childhood mementos that I held dear. I had even hung on to one of his favorite stuffed animals. David knew I had enjoyed the classic Winnie-the-Pooh—though not so much the Disney version—and had over time procured for me a plethora of classic Winnie-the-Pooh items, all of which I still possess. He had also given me a couple of the Disneyland items, one a stuffed Winnie that plays music. The younger grandkids love to play with it now.

David also knew that I loved watercolor—especially the works of the impressionists— Monet, Renoir, and Van Gogh being among my favorites. For Christmas 2001 he had purchased me a beautiful 2002 calendar with classic reproductions by several of them. This was more than a calendar with glossy pictures on cheap paper; rather, the pictures are printed on a high quality paper, and the entire piece is beautifully crafted. The year 2002 has long since passed, but the art depicted is timeless, and the calendar still hangs in my entryway. David had known me so well, and his knowing continues to make me smile.

I wasn't prepared for what I found next. When I caught sight of his familiar handwriting I wept for what seemed to be a very long time. What I had happened upon was powerful, beautiful, and telling, the reflections of a young man who thought deeply and found delight in expressing those thoughts via pen and paper. This renewed outpouring of grief over his death caught me by surprise as once again the hot tears flowed. I wanted to scream, aware that my voice wouldn't have been heard. I was already screaming from the inside. Perhaps I was too fearful of the consequences of allowing myself to do so aloud.

What I had found, tucked away in his high school writing folder, was a worn sheet of notebook paper. Nearly twelve years had passed since the time of writing. David had composed for me a Mother's Day poem in May 1993. His words carried me now to a place of gratitude for the rediscovery of his poem, but at the same time to a place of deepest grief that went beyond a longing for another dream of him to a yearning for David himself, this son in the flesh, to be with us once again. Unfolding the timeworn paper, I began to read:

*The Water*
*Peaceful water*
*Body of water*
*Joy Full water*

*Water stopped*
*The great body*
*Now a great lake*
*In a far off distance*
*The two trees*
*As new body of water and new life*
*Creek*
*The Creek from the Lake*
*A new beginning from the Lake*
*The Lake nurturing the Creek*
*The Creek turning into a beautiful Stream*
*The Stream getting its needs*
*After the fire*
*During the fire*
*Still the Lake was able*
*Able to give what the Stream needed*
*The Stream*
*The Lake*
*No matter how, when the next fire will be*
*The Lake will always be able to give back to the Stream*
*Always meeting each others needs*
*The Stream, now a great River*
*The great Lake*
*When the Lake is low the River will always give back*
*to what the Lake gave to it.*
*Love, David*

# Chapter 7

# Turning Fifty

*"Lament is an expression of tenacious faith in the midst of great and troubling sorrow. Lament says I will not give up on you even when it seems my whole world has been rocked and shattered."*

—Marilyn Weisenburg, journal entry, 2007

My fiftieth year was imprinted with extreme highs and lows. The highest high was a wedding celebration on the Oregon Coast, while the lowest low was incomprehensible and crushing. The year was marked by life-changing shifts.

On the Christmas prior to my fiftieth we were all together as a family. David had a brief leave for the holidays from his deployment training at Fort Hood in Texas. Our kids were all still single.

After that point life accelerated when Jason announced his engagement to Cindy, and their wedding was planned for the following January. Jim and I were caught up in the whirlwind of making speedy arrangements for our family to witness their vows in Las Vegas. Jason, who was in his second deployment status with the Marines, deeply desired to marry his best friend before heading out for another tour. Thankfully, the tour was scratched after the wedding.

Everyone except David was able to make it to Las Vegas for the first Weisenburg wedding. Daniel stood up as best man for his twin brother, and Jason looked incredibly handsome in his dress blues. Marines really do have the best uniforms! We enjoyed dinner at the Bellagio and afterward snapped some pictures in the conservatory and botanical gardens. Jason and Cindy were resplendent, reminding me of Cinderella and her Prince Charming posing on a winding staircase in the conservatory.

We weren't the only ones snapping pictures of the newlyweds. Passing tourists, caught up in the spell, captured the happy couple in their own photos, until Jason became overwhelmed and wanted some fresh air. War does that to a person. A few months earlier he had been in Baghdad during the toppling of Saddam Hussein's statue, and here he was posing for wedding pictures in one of the most beautiful hotels in Las Vegas.

Beyond our family lives, I wanted to mark my fiftieth year with appreciation for my youth ministry involvement at church, for eight years of fulfilling work with high school students, for establishing relationships with them and looking forward to deepening those bonds. My job in youth ministry was all about relationships—an aspect of life on which I thrived.

Elizabeth and her best friend, Stephanie, threw me a lovely birthday celebration brunch in her new home. And it was on my birthday, in the evening before we all met for dinner, that Erik proposed to Elizabeth. Jim and I were thrilled for them. They planned their wedding around David's August leave—leaving only three whirlwind months for planning! Then, only two months later, Daniel had proposed to an ecstatic Adina on a warm summer evening in Omaha. We were delighted with the imminent growth in our family. The following Christmas would take on a much different look from our previous one. As though all of this were not enough, in the midst of wedding plans our newly constructed home was nearing completion, with a move-in date scheduled for only a month before Elizabeth's wedding.

As the vicissitudes of life would have it, however, my fiftieth year was also to be marked by loss. Jim lost his position at a company in the throes of major budget cuts, whose management decided to release some of their older— and hence more expensive—employees. We also grieved the death of Jim's mother shortly before our move. Jim and Daniel made a trip to St. Louis for her service in June.

My own health, due to my peripheral neuropathy, was deteriorating. The debilitating nerve pain in my feet, arms, and legs forced me to use a wheelchair at times when distances were challenging, and the loss of my accustomed mobility—itself a death of sorts—ushered me into a place of frustration, sadness, and grief. The ongoing pressure of Jason, and then David, serving in the military in Iraq was nearly unbearable. For close to two years I endured having one son or the other in a war zone. The war was a constant on the news and in the written media, and it seemed that no matter where I looked I was reminded of the danger to which a son was exposed.

Thankfully, it wasn't long before my husband accepted an offer with another company and launched into a new career. We moved into our newly built home and began to settle in to our new surroundings. Elizabeth and Erik were married, and David was able to take his leave and be a part of the wedding celebration by the sea.

The family pictures we planned to have taken at our daughter's wedding were a gift for which I yearned during this period of adding new members to our family. I felt as though there were an urgency to have them taken—an urgency I couldn't quite articulate. That craving deep in my gut couldn't be satisfied until we all posed together on the Railtons' deck overlooking the northern Oregon coastline.

As we gathered for the family portrait deep joy filled my heart. Yet at the same time I experienced an odd interruption of the peace and joy, accompanied as they were by nagging doubts it seemed impossible to eradicate; could this be the last time we would all pose together with such carefree oblivion? *How could I even entertain such a thought?* Living as I did with the continuing tension of having sons in a war zone, however, these thoughts had a pernicious way of creeping in, uninvited and unwelcome.

I was painfully aware all along of the reality of David's return to Iraq at the end of August. He was to return to the war zone, where it seemed as though enemies lurked in every corner. When he worked on base, he and his comrades were almost daily hustled into bomb shelters because of incoming attacks. Outside the peripheral "wire" of pseudo protection the situation was worse; their missions were extremely dangerous. The troops patrolled the streets, roads, and villages in and around Baghdad, ever on the alert for bombs and bad guys. They were also the first responders to any bombings or incidents that took place in these areas. The men in David's unit would fly in on Black Hawks and then propel out of the helicopters to be the first on the scene. The Oregon 162 had already lost several soldiers over the summer of 2004. Knowing the extreme danger of my son's job, I yearned with all my heart for his safe return home, never allowing myself to assume that he would be back. I didn't like to take his return for granted and found it hard to tolerate the spoken promises I knew to be baseless and empty: "He'll be fine!" "It'll be okay!" "He'll be home soon!" I wished that these well-meaning people would choose their words more carefully. Yes, I was eager to have those wedding pictures taken . . .

It happened that in my fiftieth year I was also studying the meaning of lament. The topic intrigued me, and I found myself curiously drawn to it. I couldn't recall ever having heard a sermon or teaching on lament but now recognized that it was woven throughout the Scriptures. From the prophets of old to the book of Psalms through to the prayers of Jesus in Gethsemane, the cries of lament resounded for the receptive ear.

I was particularly drawn to lament as I coped with my chronic nerve pain, which itself threatened to undo and defeat me. I knew I lacked the soul strength, let along the physical reserves, to withstand the unrelenting pain. Not wanting to lean on myself for the strength to persevere, I pressed in to the Father and cried out in lament, "Mercy, Lord! How long?" This random, searing pain was digging deeply with its sharp talons.

I didn't like to talk about the depth of my pain, partly because there seemed for some strange reason to be an element of shame attached to it. It seemed an uncomfortable topic of conversation for any who might be involved. There were some acquaintances who simply refused to acknowledge the severity of the disorder, who had the audacity to discount my claims with the cool observation, "You don't *look* like you're in pain." The truth was that I wasn't sure *how* I was supposed to "look." I just knew I felt lousy most of the time.

So I rarely called attention to this aspect of my situation. There were some closer friends who were not only aware of my pain but who truly cared, interceding frequently for my relief and healing. Most of the time, though, I didn't want to talk about it; I wanted simply to be "normal" and to carry on with my life. I didn't want my condition to slow me down or, in particular, to prevent me from doing my job. I also shrank from drawing attention to myself in that way. While growing up I had watched my Dad navigating chronic health issues—and clearly craving attention from his family. It had worn me out to be subjected to his recurring, and obvious, attempts to divert everyone's focus onto himself. Recalling my frustration and resentment, I had no desire to follow in his footsteps.

In my lament I pressed in to Jesus. Would He bring me some relief? It was a comfort to know that the God of the Universe was ever attuned to my cry of lament. The psalms in particular became a great source of comfort to me.

In July of 2004 we had moved into a single-story home, it being easier for me to navigate without stairs; this was shortly after I had been diagnosed with peripheral neuropathy, a degenerative nerve disease. When my neurologist gave me the diagnosis, I felt as though a life sentence of pain and suffering had been handed to me. The doctor was not encouraging about my future, painting a bleak picture that *I chose to accept,* believing that my life and surroundings would close in on me, becoming progressively smaller and more confining as the neuropathy robbed me inexorably of health and well-being. I hadn't expected this type of diagnosis while in my forties and wondered what related changes would happen within the context of my job in youth ministry.

Chronic pain had prevented me from engaging in many of the day-to-day activities I had always taken for granted, and I wrestled with my uncertain future—including my altered perspective on what it might look like for me to function as a grandmother someday. I wondered what my limits might be and felt as though I were being robbed of a future I had never previously doubted. My neurologist prescribed meds for pain management, in dosages that became stronger and stronger over the course of the next few years.

There were times when, as I grappled with the diagnosis, anger welled up within me. Holding my friend's newborn or taking a stroll along the beach took on the dimensions of huge and painful undertakings.

I became my own advocate to manage pain, actively researching other means to achieve relief. It took time and effort to conduct the research, a quest that was itself exhausting. Chronic pain is exhausting to begin with, and though youth ministry could be exhausting as well, for the most part it came as a welcome distraction. I loved my work with the young people at my church.

In spite of this difficult turn in my life situation, however, I was perceptive enough to recognize the fringe benefits (which often accrue to believers in the throes of difficulties and challenges of one kind or another). The reality of chronic pain had instilled within me a deeper empathy for others who were also hurting. It had broadened my view of those around me who, I realized, might be coping with far more severe pain than my own. Over the course of time I have encountered some wonderful people who have coped with terrible pain, chronic health issues, and permanent disabilities. And the beautiful reality is that *they* have, more often than not, encouraged *me!*

I'd also made new friends when David deployed to Iraq. I was grateful for a small group of women who entered my life in late 2003; we were a small band united to pray. Two of the women had sons deployed with David, and two others were family friends. We committed to meeting every Monday morning to pray for our sons, our families, and one another.

Together Rhonda, Jody, and I poured out our hearts in prayer over our sons. Our friends Kathleen and Amy joined us as we prayed through Psalm 91 weekly for those three soldiers in our lives, as well as for the others who were deployed. Kindly, they prayed for my healing, as well.

The stress of having two sons deploying consecutively to the war zone in Iraq was a heavy weight for me to carry, and I was grateful for these women who met together on Monday mornings. We banded as mothers and friends to press in to the Lord together. The burden we individually carried seemed a bit lighter as we linked arms for support and courage.

There was a lament on my lips as our sons experienced the horrors of war. I lamented in that I had not birthed my sons for them to fight in wars. Knowing that the Lord was with me in this time of trouble was a promise to which I clung tightly, treasuring the pledge of His Presence. I clung to the words of the prophet Isaiah exhorting me not to fear; the Lord was with me and promised to strengthen and help me. In my lament I wept and cried out to the Lord about my fears for my sons.

In 2004 my duties in youth ministry were becoming a significant physical challenge. I was grateful because the majority of my work entailed meeting with young women in my office or at home. Participating in youth activities beyond this meetings had become increasingly difficult.

As a woman who loves Jesus, I also relish studying His Word. And I thoroughly enjoy immersing myself in theology, in conversing with others about God and His Word. I began to wrestle with the old message of God's wonderful plan for my life. I wrestled with my faith and wondered about would be coming next. Would I be able to continue on with my job? My heart was crying out to know the Father in deeper, more intimate ways—not only to study who He is but to worship Him with all my heart, regardless of my circumstances. I discovered that lament had led me to a place of worship.

I worshipped the Lord and called on Him as my Rock and Refuge. I declared Him good, even when my circumstances were otherwise. Although my life was changing, God's character never does. He is good, always and invariably. I called on my faithful Father when I felt that so much in my life was unsteady and uncertain.

To study or teach students about His presence and power in the midst of pain, suffering, and the unknown was for me much more than a mental exercise. These endeavors exemplified a heartfelt stirring within me to speak about His peace, His presence, and His faithful love in the midst of trouble.

The church for which I worked was top heavy with staff, the result of two congregations having merged two years earlier, in 2002. We staff members were well aware of the potential for budget cuts a couple of years following the merger, although I felt—or at least hoped—that my position in youth ministry was relatively safe. I was the only woman on the youth staff, serving with three young men, and I held to a strong belief that the young women in our church needed a woman on staff, a philosophy I assumed to have been shared among the staff. The girls in the congregation comprised half the youth group, so it seemed reasonable and important to maintain a woman on staff, not only for the girls in the youth group but also for the female volunteers with whom I met weekly.

In early September the pastor to whom those of us on staff reported summoned me on a Monday for a private meeting. Since our regularly scheduled meetings were held on Tuesdays, I instinctively surmised that something was up. Having worked with this man for nearly eight years, I could read his face and understood the gravity of his tone. I sensed that we would be discussing my position, especially after having learned that two other positions on the church staff, both held by women, had been cut.

My inkling was correct: my position was indeed being eliminated. It was apparent that my boss found it painful to deliver such disappointing news to me. I learned at the same time that the part-time junior high youth pastor would be transitioning to a full-time status. I was informed that the church saw a more pressing need for a director of women's ministry and hoped to hire someone for that position in the near future. I was absolutely devastated, feeling not only that I had been robbed but that the girls in the youth group had been wronged as well.

The news was nuanced by the distinction that the church wasn't laying me off as much as eliminating the position I held. Impulsively, I asked whether I could continue my work with the students as a volunteer. I couldn't at that moment imagine my life without my work or without contact with these people in my life. I was advised that another woman who volunteered in youth ministry would be taking on some of my previous responsibilities. The message that seemed to be implicit in this revelation was confusing and hurt terribly.

I questioned myself about the intensity with which I regarded my work. Was I idolizing it? Did I love the work I did for God more than I loved Him? As I wrestled and wept before the Lord the following week, a hymn I loved kept playing over and over again in my mind: "My Hope is Built on Nothing Less . . ." Little did I realize that at a later time the lyrics of this hymn would touch me in an even deeper way.

Indeed, I felt as though I were being enveloped by a sinkhole, just as these lyrics suggested. My grief over losing my job at the same time I was incrementally losing more and more of my health seemed nearly too much to bear. Needless to say, my angst was compounded immeasurably by the ever-present knowledge that our son was functioning day to day in a war zone in Iraq. I cried out to the Lord, lamenting the heaviness in my heart.

I firmly believe that, in the midst of an ever-changing world, Jesus is the only One to whom I can cling and of whom I can be sure. Even at that low point I trusted and believed in Him, confident that He would be with me as I ventured tentatively into a new season in my life.

It was only one short week after my position at church had been wrested from beneath me that the two uniformed soldiers made their way down our driveway, parked their car, and walked through our door to deliver the worst possible news about our son. What I had thought was too much to bear with regard to my work and health suddenly took a back seat to a parent's most dreaded and unbearable sorrow.

*Chapter 8*

# Holidays and Celebrations

The holidays were approaching and it seemed unnatural, unkind, and unimaginable to plan anything without including David. How would we navigate them as a family? Not only was David absent from our family celebrations, but we had two, and soon to be three, new family members. The dynamics had been so different a year earlier—it had been the six of us, and though wedding bells were expected, no one was as yet engaged to be married. I reminded myself to breathe slowly, unable to fathom meeting the holidays with joyful celebrations.

Soon, in early December, Jim and I would also be flying off to Maui to celebrate our thirtieth anniversary, thanks to our generous kids. This getaway, and even the planning and preparation, would be a reprieve from the chill and darkness. We had celebrated our thirtieth in August, four days prior to Elizabeth's wedding. It had been a low-key event, consumed as we were with wedding preparations. Unbeknownst to us at that time, our kids intended to honor us with some plans of their own for us to enjoy—plans of which we would remain unaware until after David's death. Only a few days after that tragic interlude in our lives, they had presented us with their generous gift, tickets to Maui for use in early December.

The tickets had been purchased in August, when David was home on leave. Now, only months later, making plans for Maui was a welcome distraction in the midst of unrelenting heartache.

A few weeks prior to Veterans Day in 2004 we received a letter from Milwaukie High School near Portland, requesting our presence, as parents of a fallen soldier, at their Veterans Day assembly and events. We sent back a card affirming that we would gather with them to remember. We were unaware at the time of their history of recognizing veterans with high regard, of their setting aside a day for classes to be taught by veterans, along with assemblies and acknowledgments. Only two months after David's passing we were wondering what the day would hold.

We were told that other parents of fallen soldiers from Oregon would be in attendance as well and that the full group would gather before the assembly. Upon our arrival Jim and I walked up and looked into their faces as introductions were made. Few words were spoken until the stories began to spill out.

We gathered around listening, affirming the pain of loss and sharing tears, hugs, and the knowing. Some of these parents and family members had been present at David's memorial service, sitting with the military personnel who had taken part. Now we met and spoke, and our stories of losing children in a war far away began to be woven together; we even learned that some of our sons had been members of the same battalion.

This was another "club" we joined—a subdivision of the less specific subculture of parents whose children had died. It didn't take long for a bonding among us to begin. We shared a common sorrow in our collective dark nights. Several of the dads stood encircled, as though protectively, around the knot of us women; few words were spoken, but the *knowing* seemed almost palpable, a shared relief and release. The moms were the storytellers, and it was at that point that a young widow joined our group, arms reaching out, holding, reassuring, loving, and protecting.

My outlook grew tremendously on this day of remembering—Veteran's Day, 2004. The young faces to go with the stories I had seen in newspapers over the past months were now imprinted on the faces of their respective loved ones. I heard about other brave soldiers who had been loved deeply and were now profoundly missed. The faces of the parents remain etched in my memory still, the deep sadness in their eyes recognized and acknowledged in the solidarity of reflecting back on our shared sorrow.

In the joining of this exclusive club we affiliated with a new family of sorts; we were alone no longer in our grief and bewilderment. Many of these men and women, themselves walking in the shadowlands of grief, had come to us in those early hours of our shock and disbelief when they had attended David's service. We had not met them at the time, but they assured us now, belatedly, that they had been there, and they spoke of the service and its particular impact on their own situations. Even the young widow had been in attendance. "This is what we do for one another, as parents and families who have lost in war. We say that we see you; we see your loved one, your pain and suffering, and we declare that you aren't alone. We attend the services whenever we can, and we remember. In this way we will honor your sons and your daughters."

Milwaukie High School goes above and beyond the merely respectable or expected to recognize a marginalized people group here in the Pacific Northwest. They recognize and honor those who have bravely served their country and ultimately given it their all. They teach well what it means to value those who have served and to perpetuate their stories. They make room to recognize the families of the fallen and to express the truth that they will not be forgotten.

On Thanksgiving an invitation was extended to the home at which the wedding had been held in August. Erik's childhood home, the setting at which he had married our daughter, would be the location of Thanksgiving for our family on this year of firsts. Pam, Erik's mom, fussed over us as she and her husband and family extended homey hospitality. We were grateful for a peaceful, neutral location affording an opportunity for new memories not fraught with painful associations. Their home, perched high on a cliff above the Pacific, offered beauty unsurpassed even along the often breathtaking northern Oregon coastline. Daniel and Adina flew in from Nebraska to be with us for the long weekend. It was tough on us to be living so far apart, and we had spoken after their June wedding about the possibility of their joint transfer to Portland State. We all recognized that they would both be so close to graduation by this point that a transfer would be complicated. Truth be told, though, there were times when I didn't know whether I could wait another year for Daniel's return to Portland. When the kids were entering their college years it had been a lot easier to let them go. Now I felt as though I could hardly breathe without each one of them being nearby. Still, I fought against the desire to be one of those clingy moms driven by irrational fear of impending loss.

Soon enough our first trip to Hawaii was upon us. I felt overwhelmed with guilt when the feelings of excitement and anticipation surfaced. Confusion abounded. How was I to reconcile my ambivalent feelings? How could we possibly enjoy the scents and sounds of a tropical vacation in the presence of the weight of grief surrounding and tempting to cripple us?

Jim would dive into tropical waters, a first experience of its kind in which he could delight. He described this experience as quiet and surreal, and the beauty as astounding. This undersea realm opened for him another world, abounding in creation's story and unfolding before his eyes, ever anew, with a startling beauty of color, depth, water, and warmth. He found himself able to let go of his grief for a while as the Pacific revealed to him, privately, a portion of its mysteries.

The warm sand under our feet soothed our souls, even as the ocean water splashed around our ankles. There was no scurrying from the gentle warmth of tropical waters as it lapped at our feet and sang to our weary hearts. The scents of jasmine and hibiscus joined the melody of God's creation and became a part of His song over us. Our heavy hearts lifted momentarily as we watched the sunrise over Haleakala and felt the gentle strokes of early morning warmth on our faces. We experienced the gentle cadence of splashing waves and found ourselves pulled into the rhythm of ebb and flow.

So far from our loved ones, we missed our family and devised a plan, sure to delight, once Daniel and Adina were married. We would bring the three married couples back with us in the coming year. They too would feel the healing waters and breathe in the fragrant scents of this faraway island. Planning this return, with them in tow, was in fact the only way we could bear being apart from them at this time. David would have loved the extravagant gift, would have wholeheartedly embraced this investment in family. It would be soothing and healing, we knew, allowing us to make new memories.

Oh, how the broken-heartedness emerged at the thought of building new memories without our oldest son. Would we be able to laugh together? Play? Could there be new joy as we strolled together in this place called paradise? Would God use this gift to ease us all into a new phase of healing and renewal as a family? Jim and I hoped the shared adventure would bond us in a new way. In another year all three of our children would be married, fresh and growing friendships within our family would be forged and deepened.

At Christmastime my cousin Jo Ann sent us the precious gift of an ornament with David's name, along with a beautiful sentiment, engraved on it. This was a time of new beginnings, of new memories to be made. We gathered in our home, a first Christmas here. The tree was raised, but much to the chagrin of our children it was a pre-lit, artificial tree. They missed the fresh pine scent, but Jim and I wanted to keep the preparations, as well as the celebration, simple.

A new tradition was forged with the ornament from Jo Ann. We would all be together once again as we hung the ornament meant to honor our son, brother, and brother-in-law. We raised our champagne glasses filled with his favorite Christmas drink, spiced eggnog. "To David. We miss you! We love you!" Glasses clinked together and silence entered. *How do we dance this dance? I'm overwhelmed with the missing of him. For twenty-six years he was among us, celebrating. He has been the gift giver par excellence in our family—the creative, thoughtful one, ever delighting in the findings that so ideally fit each personality.*

In the forthcoming Christmastimes we would learn a new dance, new ways to celebrate as a family. We would adopt the new vision held by Imago Dei Church regarding Christmas giving and become involved in the lives of those who were truly needy. We would extend the love of Christ and make it less about us and more about Him. It would be called the Advent Conspiracy—our church would spearhead a movement of love and celebrating in a new way we had never before experienced.

That would be in the future, but today, in 2004, our Christmas felt hollow at times, and even foreign. Our grief was so fresh and still so raw. The missing of David overruled and threatened to undo me. Would gravity continue to hold me down, disallowing my spirit to soar unfettered? Would the pain of a raging, chronic nerve disease drive me to despair? Would I be able to voice, and willing and desirous to convey, my fear and grief? And, now that my job had run its course, would the lies concerning my perceived devaluation drag me down into the pit? Or would my ears hear and acknowledge the truth? As I wrestled and wondered and lamented to my Father in heaven, would He show up? Would He break through this pain, or would He remain so seemingly silent and distant, so far away, and perhaps so disinterested . . . ?

God was the only One who could save me from sinking into helpless despair. How far would I descend before the hand of my Father would pluck me up out of the muck and save me? *How long, Jesus? How long will this raw aching go on?*

# Chapter 9

# Uncomfortable

Belonging to a group within our larger church structure provided us with a sense of community. Going to church and participating in church life and youth ministry were what we had been about for fifteen years at this church. Obviously, our church was a major part of our lives. We had raised our children in this place, and they were known and loved here, as were we. However, the situation had become complicated, confusing, and awkward now that my position in youth ministry had been eliminated and another woman was doing the work on a volunteer basis. It felt as though there was no room for me after eight years of serving, and this major change in my life was complicating my grief in numerous ways.

Some decisions that had been made in the youth department hurt me deeply, and it went without saying that we were grieved beyond words over David's death. Overwhelmed and conflicted, we stopped attending church altogether for a while. We weren't giving up on God, but I was tired of our particular church and of answering questions about how I felt about the changes. Church politics were making me ill.

Some people would approach me about the fact that not one but three women had been laid off, but I lacked the energy reserves to address the gender issue in their presence. My loss of David was, it went without saying, infinitely deeper than that of my job. I knew that we were loved by many of the people there, but the aggravated situation regarding the job loss was confusing and disheartening.

Putting a hold on church attendance for a while would, we reasoned, allow us to catch our breaths, not to mention that the very effort to get ready and go out on Sunday mornings with our game faces on had become too much. To finally arrive at church and then be confronted by questions on the congregation's political front was painfully awkward and, given our limited reserves, simply too much to bear.

Occasionally we would visit other churches, where we preferred to remain anonymous most of the time. Jim and I could walk into a new congregation, not knowing a soul. This would feel a little strange, but the atmosphere felt less stifling, as though we had room to breathe a bit. On the down side, walking into a church and later back out without being known left us isolated, and I started to feel lonely for the high school students and the youth staff. At one church we visited I wandered out of the service while the pastor was teaching and followed the sound of young people singing. Finding a large classroom filled with young people and standing unobserved in the back of the room left me with an unbearable sadness. I was missing the presence of the particular students with whom I had worked, as well as, more generally, my position and function in youth ministry.

We both began to miss our home church and the people there whom we loved, and we eventually found our way back to the church at which I had lost my job—back to where our friends were. It felt odd, however, to enter in without being involved on our accustomed level, and making the transition back was tough and complicated. We talked often about the possibility of moving on, praying about it and asking God for His help and direction. Although we did speak with our grief counselor several times about the possibility of leaving our church, we were aware that it is neither easy nor wise to make a high-impact decision during a period of intense grief. In fact, most counselors will caution against making any major decisions when deeply grieving. Ours cautioned us several times, though he understood why we would lean in the direction of changing our congregational affiliation. We ultimately made the decision once again to "take a break" and began visiting our daughter and son-in-law's church, Imago Dei Community.

We liked the overall sense of this church as a place where broken people were invited in, received, and loved. We both love and appreciate worship songs with deep, rich meaning and found this style of music here. The songs were like a balm poured over our broken hearts, even during those times when we found it beyond our ability to sing along or even form the words on our lips. We appreciated our new pastor, Rick McKinley, and the manner in which he spoke about truth, hope, and redemption. Would ours be a redemption story, I began to wonder? When Rick spoke I began to wonder whether my heart would ever be hopeful again, though Rick's words of hope for the broken began to ever so slightly mend my broken heart.

We felt safe at Imago Dei, however, even as we felt lonely and sad, missing the students and friends, both in youth ministry and beyond, in our previous church. At Imago we rarely saw or met anyone our own age, and we had few friends there in 2005, though knowing and seeing many of Elizabeth and Erik's friends at church was lovely. A few of David's friends attended there as well, and it was a comfort to meet them and to partake with them in communion together. We began to feel at home at Imago and decided to make a commitment to become a part of the church.

One Sunday after we had attended Imago for a few weeks, our pastor, Rick, and two other elders approached us. I don't recall which one initiated the conversation, but the three walked toward us together, their heads humbly bowed. Their demeanor spoke to me of an unusual tenderness, a consideration of parents in grief, and they mutually expressed sorrow over our loss. Although they acknowledged that they couldn't imagine what we were going through, they made clear that they would have no expectations of us—no intention, for example, of asking one or the other of us to lead this or that group. They just wanted us *to be*. How comforting it was to hear this from them. They offered no churchy words, religious platitudes, or simple answers, nor did they regale us with the slap of a verse on our wound with the intention of making it all better. Their humility was genuine, and it encouraged our hearts deeply.

At home my heart was softening as I read and meditated on Lamentations 3, a passage I felt to be imprinted on my heart: "*Because of His great love we are not consumed . . .*" This launched me into a sense of the scope of the Lord's amazing grace for me. As I wrestled, the pain of loss still unrelenting, I became amazed anew by the grace He was pouring out on me—the gift of a mercy that allowed me room in which to struggle. The door that had seemed to be shut so tightly between the Lord and me began to crack open through this unmistakable extension of His grace. I sensed His nearness even as I faced my sorrow head on. My confidence in the Lord was growing. He was with me in my brokenness and wouldn't let me go. He was breaking through the fog of grief with a grace much greater than my pain and sorrow. When words were spoken that could have deeply discouraged me, I asked for His grace to cover me and prevent me from falling into despair.

In the course of visiting with some friends with whom I had previously worked, I also saw and visited with a retired pastor. God's grace covered me in that context, too, as we talked . . . and as I was unexpectedly assaulted by his thoughtless words. This man asked me how I was doing, and I replied honestly that "sometimes I'm up and sometimes I'm down." I have no doubt I could have given a much more satisfactory answer, but these were the words that tumbled from my mouth. I wished I had articulated something eloquent about the waves of grief. Still, I was unprepared for his reply: "Marilyn! I thought you had more strength and character than that!" Stunned and chagrined, I mumbled something in return. Soon after speaking with him I made my exit and left for home, chewing on his words and asking questions of myself out loud. "What was his purpose in shaming me? Will shame guide me to the arms of God?" It appeared as though I somehow embodied a disappointment to this man. I was thankful I probably wouldn't run into him again.

Two women sent me letters consistently. One older woman from our previous church wrote to me often to let me know she was thinking of me and praying. I had never met her, but she wrote regardless, impelled by her love and concern. She wrote because she too had experienced great loss, that of her husband. She wrote often, to lift up my broken heart. Another woman lived out of state; I had earlier worked with her son-in-law in youth ministry. She would reminisce about her walks on the beach on the central coast of California and share how the Lord would guide her to pray for me. She would write out the words of the prayer she had been praying, put the note in an envelope, and send it my way. I loved reading her words and basking in my knowledge of how the Lord was moving her to pray. I loved receiving her handwritten notes, which were loving and personal in tone. These letters constituted God's grace-song over me.

I believed that His grace was greater than all of my anger but still found myself amazed that He could be so patient, so full of longsuffering for me as I wrestled with confusion, hurt, grief, and rancor. I was an angry mess—furious at war, at death, and at terrorists and their horrific brutality. I was enraged with people who thought it was okay to inform me, uninvited, of their insider insight that everything I had endured was part of God's plan.

"If it happened, it must be His will."

Or "David's in heaven now; you'll see him again."

"God always takes the best first."

"God needed David in heaven."

"At least he was there for your daughter's wedding—be thankful!"

Or, after a short few months had passed, "Are you doing better now?"

I was enraged at the messed up theology that was being expressed to me, even while I understood that some people were uncomfortable with my grief and anger.

One deep layer of that grief had to do with my processing of *how* David had died. Jim knew the details—information that I, at this stage, could neither hold nor bear. I knew the brief account, but the details were too much. When I thought about those moments, I felt as though I could hardly breathe. His death, despite having been instantaneous, had been brutal and violent, and I simply couldn't wrap my head around what had happened to him. I would ask Jim to assure me again and again that David had died instantly, that he hadn't suffered. At the height of those instances in which I struggled acutely with his death, I felt myself seething with anger.

What we had gone through as parents, coupled with our inability to view our son's body, remained tough to process, terribly difficult to navigate. Simplistic answers and religious platitudes, far from being a comfort, felt dismissive.

The perception of our sorrow and pain being like a switch we could just flip off because a stranger saw fit to apprise us that we'll "see him in heaven" was incredible. Nor could we simply paste on an act of having it all together. What had happened to our beloved son was simply not okay, nor was his death a provision of the divine plan. War is never okay, any more than are violence, hatred, greed, or murder.

One man asked me a pointed personal question about ten months after David's death. Sitting next to me and opening a conversation, he took the liberty of asking, "Marilyn, why are you still so angry? Who are you angry with?" I took a deep breath, which I slowly and deliberately let out before answering: "I'm angry because terrorists violently took my son's life. I can't wrap my head around it. I think about it all the time. I am deeply grieved." To this day I remain uncertain he had the capacity to understand.

Another time this same man—a pastor—caught sight of me in passing. On this day, at this time, when he asked how I was doing I responded honestly that I was doing fairly well. My grief could hit me like crashing waves at times, while at other times it flowed more gently. Visibly relieved, he began compulsively patting me on the back and repeating, "Keep on doing well, Marilyn. Keep on doing well."

I recognized immediately his level of discomfort with my pain—and quite possibly, I surmised, with all hurt and brokenness. He shied away from the broken stories, not wanting to hear about the hopelessness and despair that were screaming at me, tempting me to surrender. Perhaps it was terrifying for him to find himself unable to control a situation or outcome, at a loss for words and answers. Perhaps he felt ill equipped to help the hurting.

At another time I was in a large group of women at a wedding shower, when I encountered a woman I had known from years earlier, when our children were young. She and I had once participated in a Bible study together. She knew my story, and it was clear that she was uncomfortable seated across from me. She asked me cheerfully, "Are you keeping busy, Marilyn?" to which I smiled and replied, "Umm, actually, no . . . I'm not keeping super busy. I probably could have stayed busy if I still had my job, but no. Now I'm purposely not doing busywork because I'm trying to work hard in facing my grief."

At an obvious loss to formulate a response, she nervously looked away. I understood that responses like this made some people uncomfortable. *But how else*, I asked myself in frustration, *should I be responding at this point in my story? Do they want me to smile and say everything is just great and add a nice sounding religious cliché? Would that make people feel more comfortable? Or should I just stay away from meetings, celebrations, studies, and such till I can honestly say I'm doing "better"?*

After those and several other awkward conversations, I began to perceive just how uncomfortable some within the church really are in the presence of grief. Such an individual would, no doubt, much rather have me smile and assert brightly that everything was "just fine." Finding it painful to acknowledge, let alone confront, grief and pain, they would rather see the hurting quick-stepping their way through the maze of sadness and carrying on. They'd rather see us pick ourselves up, saunter into church with renewed vigor, and join in the singing of those happy, clappy styles of song on a Sunday morning.

*I began to see that oftentimes people are simply uncomfortable with being uncomfortable. And we're no different in that regard from those outside the church. What won't we do to avoid, stuff, or assuage the pain and suffering we all carry? We drink, eat, shop, and work too much. We use, abuse, cut, view porn, play endless online games, and compulsively throw ourselves into a multitude of church activities. We do all we can, at a frenetic pace, to pursue that elusive state touted as happiness. We do whatever it takes to deny or dismiss pain and loss.* In my own story, I could avoid the pain for an hour while I shopped like a mad woman, but out in my car, alone once again, I would burst into tears as reality seeped into my awareness once again. It is embedded in our Western culture to encourage the denial of pain.

When will we stop tossing out simple answers? When will we stop repeating religious clichés and platitudes? Why do we try to wrap it all up and top it with a neat little bow? When will we stop talking and strutting about as though we have all the answers?

As I confronted my grief and pain and thought about these odd and ineffective responses to the grieving, questions emerged. A theme of denial stood out for me. I wondered about the overall level of denial of feelings within the church. I wondered whether some churchgoers are unacquainted with their own feelings or fear vulnerability to the point of lacking the courage to acknowledge and confront their own losses. I know that I struggled against these very issues in the past, raised as I was to deny or minimize negative feelings and soldier on. When I experienced my deepest grief I recognized that this same attitude has permeated the church culture.

We desperately need Jesus—for every step we take and every breath we breathe. We need Him as we navigate life's vicissitudes and face our inevitable losses. When we do suffer loss, will we have the courage to authentically grieve and lament? Or will we try to bury our pain deep down and carry on as though we're unaffected?

When we refuse to lament our losses we are in effect declaring our independence from the One called Emmanuel, God with us. We're glibly asserting, "I don't need you, Lord.

I've got this one—it's okay. I'm blessed in so many ways, so I'm supposed to smile and carry on, right?"

He is our Creator. That means that He has designed us and is mindful of our emotions. When we attempt to bury or stuff them, we trick ourselves into believing that we have those pesky, unreliable feelings under control, and we begin to operate under our own presumed strength, donning a smiling mask and keeping our chins up. Eventually, though, our pain finds an out in one way or another.

We might know theoretically that Jesus is our Comforter, Healer, Prince of Peace, and Redeemer. But do we acknowledge this when the winds blow hard against us? When we experience loss beyond our comprehension? When 280,000 people are swept away by a tsunami or when a classroom of trusting six-year-olds is brutally mowed down by gunfire?

If we choose to bury our angst, we pass up the opportunity to know with confidence, even in the midst of excruciating loss, that He truly loves us and that he IS WITH US. His Presence is His promise in the midst of trouble, isn't it? Why would we avoid this kind of intimacy with Him? Why do we fear lamenting our grief?

Clark and Cathy recently returned from living in Uganda for nearly a year, and I have listened to many of their stories. We were talking about grief the other day, and they described how the people in the village in which they lived openly express their grief when a loved one dies. The death rate there is high, with this passage an expected aspect of everyday life.

The climate is hot in Adjumani, which is near the equator, and it's a welcome relief when the night breeze wafts its refreshment. One evening when the air was a bit cooler Cathy was sitting outside in their front yard, when suddenly she heard a woman's piercing wails of sorrow. Down the road from where they lived yet another person in their village had died. Cathy's heart grieved for her neighbor. Hearing her keening wails echoing in the night hours led her to tears of her own, as well as to intercession to the Father of mercies and the God of all comfort to be with the grieving ones. She appreciated the honesty of the emotions of people she knew to be mourning. They didn't put on a false front, grit their teeth, and soldier on, didn't insist that everything was just fine, that they would after all one day see their departed loved one again in glory. They didn't simply keep on keeping on. They were honest about their sorrow and about the extent to which their loved one would be missed.

This story from Uganda made me yearn for us, self-reliant individualists that we are, to be honest about our own feelings when confronted with loss—honest with our pain, as opposed to independently picking ourselves up by our own boot straps and carrying on, seemingly without missing a beat.

Why do we feel it necessary to put on a brave front? Why is it applauded when we're able to sit through the memorial service or funeral of a loved one without shedding a tear?

A friend's cousin related a story of their aunt's "bravery" at her own daughter's memorial service. The cousin asserted that she was so proud of the aunt for keeping a stiff upper lip and not breaking down in tears, and my friend was incredulous upon hearing this account of her cousin's memorial service. When she related it to me, everything in me screamed *NO!!!!* Please don't foist your expectations of dry eyes and a stiff upper lip on someone who has lost a child. They're in deep pain and sorrow and need your understanding and patience, not your judgment if they weep over the loss of their son or daughter, no matter what age they are.

The mercy gift of the Lord's grace allowed me to be honest in my wrestling before Him. I can't imagine a faith that would require me to put on a smile and affirm with demure resolve that "this is all a part of His plan" when my son was brutally killed. How could I smile and carry on when I wasn't so much as permitted to view his body— mutilated though it may have been—when it was returned home for burial? Of course I wrestled with my faith.

I received a God-given gift, however, as I wrestled: I experienced God's grace in the midst of it. He took me to a place where I could sincerely recite David's inimitable words in the shepherd psalm, even while in the throes of suffering. He is a God full of mercy, grace, compassion, and goodness, and what's more . . . He loves me. It was never His intention or design for war and its violence to take out my son. For that matter, it isn't His intention, based on some grand plan, for death to claim anyone, in war or whatever other scenario. Why would He use the evil He hates to accomplish His purposes?

In the midst of all my grappling, in the midst of my wandering in this wilderness of pain, suffering, and loss, I recognized that His grace, mercy, and compassion constitute for me a wide open space. He, the longsuffering God, the God who Himself groans for our pain, is full of lovingkindness and goodness.

We typically hear the declaration "God is good!" when a follower of Christ receives something special or something wonderful happens. A new job is secured: "God is good!" A home is sold and a new one purchased: "God is good!" A loved one is declared cancer-free: "God is good!" Someone lands that coveted parking space, and, even then, "God is good!"

How often, though, do we hear that declaration when one is unemployed or homeless for months, or a little one battling cancer is released from her mother's arms for yet another round of chemotherapy? The proclamation, while certainly true, seems rather unfitting—or at least ill timed—does it not? And yet we concur that God is indeed good and that His goodness is in no way dependent upon our life circumstances.

A good and mighty God has given me space to grieve and lament the death of my son.

What would I uncover as I entered the ancient path of lament? What was His intention in giving me the gift of the shepherd psalm, nestled unobtrusively there in His Word? Could it be that He was asking me to make lament in a familiar and comfortable language, rather than assuming this genre to be the exclusive property of the skeptics, cynics, and complainers? I believe that in the redemption piece of my loss and pain He was ushering me in to the beauty of the sanctified song of lament. In Psalm 23 and other such Old Testament gems He bequeathed to me a venue through which I could honestly, forthrightly, and still worshipfully speak to Him of my sorrow. It would have been utterly incongruous for me to paint a smile on my face and then attempt, through gritted teeth and squeezed eyelids, to worship in truth. I couldn't in those circumstances and in that frame of mind have resonated with happy, clappy songs, nor could I have mouthed song lyrics proclaiming pious promises to Him. It was specifically the vehicle of lament that led me to worship and extol His worthiness. He met me in the place of authentic sorrow before Himself and guided me gently to His declaration in Lamentations 3:33, "*For He does not willingly bring affliction or grief to the children of men.*"

My Father was indeed breaking through my anger and fog of grief with a grace infinitely beyond and greater than my pain and sorrow, to that place of grace wherein I could know, experientially and confidently, that He is with me, loves me, and instills within me the courage to face and express my grief.

# Chapter 10

# Arlington National Cemetery

Our collective stories brought us to Washington, DC, in the spring of 2005. We, the families and loved ones of fallen soldiers, were invited by Annette Polan, the founder of Faces of the Fallen, to visit a memorial to the more than 1,300 men and women who had died in the wars in Iraq and Afghanistan. Annette, Professor Emeritus from the Corcoran College of Art and Design, is a portrait artist and a visionary who conceived the idea after having been inspired by newspaper photos and their accompanying stories. She gathered more than 200 volunteer artists, who together designed an exhibit for the purpose of bringing us all together.

Annette explained on NPR radio that she wanted to give our families something more permanent than a fleeting image in a newspaper. She emphasized to each artist involved in the exhibit that they had a mission, through the power of art, to honor the fallen and offer some measure of comfort and closure to their families.

Each portrait was to be eight inches tall and six inches wide, though the uniform size was her only stipulation. The result was a wide-ranging collection of works in glass and fiber, woodcarvings, drawings and illustrations, paintings, collage, and montage. Some were three-dimensional. In all, more than 1,300 portraits were included. The exhibit was so popular that its timeframe was extended several times. It opened for an exclusive showing to the families and friends of the fallen on Tuesday, March 22, 2005, at Arlington National Cemetery. The following day it would be open to the public.

Jim and I received a letter from Annette months before the exhibit was to open, personally inviting us to be present. We didn't hesitate about attending, immediately booking tickets for the two of us, along with Jason and Cindy. We understood that at least 2,000 family members and friends of fallen soldiers would be in attendance.

Later on we listened to a phone message left by the ABC television network, requesting an interview after we had viewed David's portrait. Jim and I discussed this invitation at length. We were both wary of granting interviews, although this time we were not hasty in declining. In the end we agreed to conduct the interview on the morning of the opening day, before the door was opened to the rest of the families. We were grateful for the private time and space allotted to us as we looked for David's portrait among the 1,300 plus exhibited.

The four of us walked the long, narrow education hall at Arlington National Cemetery, spotting David's likeness at last and then gazing, transfixed, on the artist's rendering of our son's handsome face. The artist had used the picture Elizabeth had snapped of David and me right after his arrival in Cannon Beach for her wedding—the same one that had appeared in the newspapers. He was wearing civilian clothes, including his well-worn signature red jacket, which still today hangs in our coat closet at home. His enormous smile dominates the picture as he beams at his sister.

It was beautifully drawn, and we stared for a very long time, as though we couldn't get enough of it. Jason and Cindy were both moved to tears, as were Jim and I. Who would have thought that our David's portrait would be featured in an outstanding exhibit of this nature, at Arlington National Cemetery? We held each other and wept, continually repeating to each other how grateful we were for the privilege of walking into the exhibit early and cherishing some private moments.

Annette greeted us warmly before introducing us to the woman with whom we had corresponded for the interview with ABC. We were struck by the respect and kindness flowing from Annette to us.

We spoke with ABC briefly. We were asked about David, what he had been like, what branch of the military he had been in, and what he had wanted to do upon his return from Iraq. "Does this help the healing process, the recovery?" they asked. We answered honestly: yes it did, though we were still numb in our grief. Brief as the interview was, it left us emotionally spent. We said our goodbyes and viewed once again our David's portrait, still within the quiet time so thoughtfully reserved for ourselves alone. We took pictures and looked for the portraits of the sons of other Oregon parents we had recently met. Depleted, we decided to leave for a while before the exhibit officially opened for the rest of the families and friends.

We drove to the Tomb of the Unknown Soldier and were present when the military guards changed positions. This was a solemn moment of remembering—of honoring—and I was grateful for the opportunity to set my eyes on this sacred ground. Later we viewed the famous Iwo Jima Memorial statue, along with many others. Jason was especially moved by the Iwo Jima statue, and we snapped pictures of him and Jim in front of it.

Upon our return we encountered a changed scene. A group was gathering near the door of the education hall. Typically, when crowds wait for an exhibit to open there is chatter, laughter, and merriment. This opening was different; this wasn't just an event. It was as though we were all being ushered in together, families and friends, into a solemn service—into a memorial service, a time to gather, reflect, remember, and weep as one. Even as the crowd swelled there was a holy hush within its growing numbers. We spoke in whispers, if at all. We were about to set foot within a sacred place, and all knew it.

When the doors opened there was no rushing ahead, no breaking rank to push or jockey for position, to be first inside. Some were hesitant and reluctant. Would they be pleased with the artist's rendition of their beloved fallen soldier? Others were cautious, perhaps self-conscious or emotionally overcome, with eyes averted. We took our time, allowing others to file in ahead of us. We had already had our time. We could wait—knowing at the same time that our place was among these people, the company of the grieving.

Because it was difficult for me to stand for long periods of time, we rented a wheelchair that Jim pushed. Waited until the crowd had shuffled its way inside, we entered once again. David's portrait, we knew, was near the end on the opposite side. The large crowd filled the narrow hall, leaving little space to navigate the wheelchair. Still, despite the press, it was very quiet, holy.

A tall and distinguished looking man wearing a black leather jacket stood before us, searching for his son's portrait. Jim quietly excused himself, and the man turned and widened the way for us. As we passed he looked at Jim straight in the eyes, and Jim looked back. They knew. They knew they were both fathers who had lost children to war. They stood facing each other without speaking and warmly shook hands. I will never forget those kind yet sorrowful eyes. I will never forget the reciprocity of the mutual knowing. I will never forget the lack of pretense in this unique and exclusive gathering.

There were more moments like this—the knowing looks and understanding eyes, . . . and the raw sobs. A young woman, barely twenty, stood in the back weeping with her brother. A young widow, overcome. Grief unspeakable.

We found David's portrait once again. After a while another family nearby quietly asked, "Your son?" And we spoke the stories of our sons together. There were more stories shared, with people we had never met before, encounters anonymous and yet intimate. We told the stories that broke our hearts, that cut within us a fresh, deep wound in the retelling. Love spoken, respect and honor given and reciprocated in kind. We were the ones left behind. We grieved anew over sons and daughters, sisters, brothers, and spouses. This seemed to be the appropriate place and time to be vulnerable with our stories, to empathize mutually, without worrying about reaction or dodging sympathy or unwanted attention. Some spoke of emotions so raw they couldn't bring themselves to utter a follow-up word. Others spoke of a grandmother still too grief-stricken to face this memorial. For those who could and would speak, we talked about the honoring. And we grieved together. Our stories were a bridge to connect and receive without self-consciousness or a fear of standing out as conspicuous or different. There was a holy compassion poured out—mercy received and given in the telling. Our loved ones wouldn't be forgotten.

Later on we gathered once again, outside near a fountain. A stage was set and chairs assembled for the crowd. We would hear from Annette as she told her story and spoke of her vision for our loved ones. Dignitaries were in attendance. The diminutive Justice Sandra Day O'Connor, her presence large despite her physical compactness, walked up to the platform, as did senators and military personnel. There were many speeches, a dedication, and a song. The Chairman of the Joint Chiefs of Staff, Air Force Gen. Richard B. Myers, was the keynote speaker, and he and his wife shook hands and took pictures with many of the families afterward. We heard later read an article written by Jim Garamone in The American Forces Information Service that General Meyers was "the last to leave the hallowed ground of Arlington on this special day."

We made room for new friends from Oregon. Families, no longer strangers, were sitting side by side. We wept together, told our stories, and hoped. We hoped for one another as our wounded souls inched along in the process of healing. We weren't alone. We belonged to a larger family and sensed in a hitherto unprecedented manner the power and solidarity of belonging. How powerful it was to be together!

In our room back at the hotel, Jim and I marveled over the day. What a privilege and honor to travel here, to be a part of this moment that was like no other. We had few words. And we were weary, craving some rest before we headed out for another couple of days of sightseeing with Jason and Cindy.

Embedded in our hearts were the stories, the faces, the honoring, the eyes of those left behind. We had come together for one moment of our lives, and those lives would never again be quite the same.

# Chapter 11

# Plates

As grief continued to hang over me like a threatening storm cloud, I grew progressively more and more weary. Gazing out the window at the pouring rain, I recalled a time months earlier when I had stood looking out the deck door into a torrential downpour. This memory stemmed from two days prior to David's memorial service, and I remember thinking how surreal it was that we would so soon be attending a memorial service for the son who still seemed so vital in our memories. It was raining fast and furious, typical in the Northwest. The other detail I remember clearly is that I was alone for the first time since receiving the news of David's passing. No one was visiting, and Jim had gone out to run a quick errand. I wept soundlessly from deep inside my soul, uncomfortable at the thought of my voice being heard.

I glanced, as though with a start, at the deck again because something had caught my eye. When it rains this hard in the Pacific Northwest I'm invariably drawn to the torrent. Yet today there was something unusual about it— what appeared to be an even heavier deluge, within the larger body of the downpour, over a section of the deck. I've lived in the Northwest all my life and have never seen such torrential rain, either before or after this incident. It was at that moment that I understood: although I was alone in my home, the Presence of God was with me, and He was making Himself known in a mighty and unforgettable way. He was weeping with me—his own Father tears unabashed and unabated.

Thinking back on that day, I reflected upon the Lord, the One who is called the Author of Life. I knew that David's early death wasn't a part of His plan or intention, that He doesn't work through evil to accomplish His purposes. I also acknowledged that He had the power to intervene and yet did not. Nor did He step in to prevent my best friend's succumbing to cancer, or the abuse of someone I loved. No, He didn't plan for these horrible things to happen, but He could have put a stop to the travesty, . . . so why didn't He? I was overwhelmed by this God of Mystery, all the while knowing that I was powerless to "figure Him out" or try to make sense of such tragedy. I couldn't reason any of this out. It just was. I couldn't fathom a redemption story coming out of this—at least in terms of the short-term outcome that seemed so ultimate. It was with this that I wrestled. Would this God of Mystery mark my story with His grace and His touch? In a way that I could identify, and in which I could find comfort? I believed that He would, but what would that look like?

Jim and I began meeting with a grief counselor three weeks after David died. Every session began with the same desperate, pleading questions:

*How long . . . ?*
*How long will the raw pain last?*
*How long will we live and breathe this crushing sadness?*
*Will we ever laugh again?*
*Will we ever again experience joy?*
*Is this normal?*

Our counselor affirmed that our feelings were normal, that the rawness and shock would likely last a year or so. I wondered anxiously: *How can I not breathe again for a whole year?* I was overcome by the question of how I could bring myself to enter into the joy of two more wedding celebrations in our family. They were coming up so soon. Jason and Cindy's wedding reception was planned for April, with Daniel and Adina's wedding was scheduled for a few weeks later, in early June.

Both couples had set these dates while David was in Iraq. Both had wanted to wait for his return, had wanted him to be present with the rest of our family. But David wasn't coming home. The family dynamic had abruptly and completely changed. I grieved for our surviving sons as they attempted to balance their grief over David against their joy in upcoming marriages.

I agonized over how I would move forward and enter into the more imminent celebration, that of Jason and Cindy. Would I then be too overwhelmed for Daniel and Adina's wedding? I wanted all of them to know how happy I was for them and their decision to marry. There was such tension in my heart, not the least of which involved the need to celebrate as a family minus an essential member. Only by God's grace, I knew, would I find the strength be present and joyful for these soon-to-be wedded couples. I knew I would need Him every moment, that I couldn't possibly manage in my own strength, and I pleaded with the Lord for His help, all the while wishing I could simply retire to my bed and stay there.

My internal struggles didn't always match my outward appearance. I made the deliberate choice to rise in the mornings and face each day. Perhaps at that point my friends may have surmised that I was managing, but my ever-escalating anger remained just beneath the surface.

Dancing with Jason at his wedding reception afforded me an opportunity to express my love to him, as well as my joy at sharing this momentous occasion with my son. I was grateful that he was with us, home from that wretched war. Safe. Moments later, however, a slideshow played and I noticed tenderhearted Daniel in the wings, drawing us all as near to himself as possible—our family minus one. In fact, he verbalized his wish to gather us all in his arms, making it a little softer and safer for each of us as we watched the slideshow of Jason and Cindy's young lives playing out before us. He has shared my difficulty in viewing family photos since David's death.

The following June Daniel and Adina were married in Omaha, Nebraska. Another family wedding in Omaha had been planned for one week prior to theirs, so I flew out early to attend that celebration. My cousin's daughter was marrying an Army soldier, and he wore dress blues.

I resisted the triggers, deliberately practicing presence and being swept up in the celebration at hand. At the reception I stood and watched the groom dancing with his radiant mama: the handsome soldier-groom, strong, sure, and steady. I smiled at them during their special moment, and then, out of nowhere, came a crashing wave of grief, an emotional tsunami nearly knocking me off my feet. I was watching them enjoy a dance that would never be mine with David. Dashing out of the reception area and into the restroom, I stood in a bathroom stall trying to muffle my tears and reminding myself to breathe. My cousin Laurie and my son Daniel both noticed and hurried in after me, providing comfort and imbuing me with the strength I would need to eventually make my way back to the reception and rejoin the celebration.

Thanks to the intercessions of many friends, I was able the following week, at Daniel and Adina's wedding, to be fully present and to celebrate with them and our family. Theirs was a deeply meaningful and beautiful wedding, with my cousin Gary officiating and Clark also playing a significant role in the ceremony. Dancing with Daniel at the reception was a moment I'll always cherish. A few weeks later at their Portland reception I sensed the Lord's nearness and was profoundly grateful for His preventing me from falling apart at a time intended for focus on the bride and groom.

Once the weddings and receptions were behind us I felt relieved of the burden of anticipation and of preparation for such intense social gatherings. As the reality of life as usual seeped back in, however, I once again longed to crawl into bed and stay there. There had been so many changes during that rollercoaster year. All three of our surviving children were now married, I no longer had a job to go to, and David wouldn't be returning home from the war zone.

I had compartmentalized my grief work for the sake of making it through the celebrations intact, but now that I was able to let down my guard the waves of grief came crashing over me with new intensity. Anger, kept momentarily at bay, now threatened to engulf me. There was nothing to distract me from the raw pain of my grief.

My counselor, Cindy, became my anchor. I was floundering and nearly sinking in the depth of my sorrow and loss, but she pulled me up, kindly and compassionately, recognizing the compounded losses I was facing and listening attentively as I spoke of my pain and bewilderment. She spoke life and hope over me, and I trusted that what she said was true, even when my feelings failed to follow suit. There *was* hope. I *would* get through this shock and pain and suffering . . . by walking through it one deliberate step at a time. I was ready to face it head on. She was with me every step of the way: Jesus' strength and healing graces, I knew, resided during that season in this woman of God.

Cindy pointed out that I had before me a labor of grief—a daunting prospect there would be no way to

*David holding Jason, Elizabeth holding Daniel, 1981*

*Weisenburg Family, 1982*

*Dad's birthday, 1985*

*David camping at Lost Lake in Oregon, 1985*

*Graham and David, ready for Awana, 1986*

*David and friend Sarah, standing in front of his beloved '64 Malibu*

*Jordan, Stephen, Jason, David, Dad, Andrew, John, 1999*

*Andrew, David, Stephen, John, traditional photo op, 1999*

*David, South Korea, 1999*

*Jason graduating from Marine Boot Camp, Camp Pendleton, 2001*

*David and Elizabeth, 2003*

*Oregon 162 Deployment Ceremony. Jon, Caleb and David, 2003*

*Christmas 2003. Standing l-r Daniel, David, Jason,*
*sitting l-r, Marilyn, Jim, Elizabeth*

*St Mary's swim team and coaches, Liane and David, 2003*

*David and the Kiowa in Iraq, 2004*

*David and Caleb in Iraq, 2004*

*David and Peter –* Oregonian *interview with Mike Francis and Ben Brink in Iraq, 2004*

*Elizabeth and Erik's wedding, August 2004*

*Elizabeth and her brothers, August 2004*

*David and Marilyn, August 2004*

*Taking a break from patrol in Iraq, 2004*

*Memorial service in Iraq for David Weisenberg and Ben Isenberg
(from the* Oregonian*), September 2004*

*Christmas 2004. Standing l-r Cindy, Elizabeth, Marilyn, Adina, sitting l-r Jason, Erik, Jim, Daniel*

*Overnighter with Papa and Meme: l-r Silas, Quinnleigh, Aubie, Lincoln, Elliott, 2015*

circumvent. I knew it was absolutely necessary to face my grief, but it would also be messy, one of the hardest things I'd ever done. We—she and I—would work through it a little at a time. One of the most pressing issues I faced was my fury. It seemed as though I just couldn't pry myself away from that war in Iraq.

Everywhere I looked there were reminders.

I saw pictures of war scenes on magazine covers in the grocery store.

I saw pictures of war scenes on magazine covers in reception rooms.

I opened the newspaper to find once again that the front page of *The Oregonian* was all about the war.

At that time an Oregon National Guard battalion was once again deployed to Iraq. It went without saying that the local newspaper would cover the stories. And when we turned on the TV the coverage would be all over both the local and national news.

The trauma had a way of hitting especially hard when I was driving. Hummers were becoming a popular vehicle at the time, and they seemed to be everywhere. I felt overwhelmed when, once again, I found myself driving behind one on the freeway. I was overwhelmed as I thought about David and Ben, inside their Hummer on patrol on September 13, 2004. I felt physically ill when I saw one on the freeway. "*Why, of all the vehicles I could drive behind, is this one in front of me?*"

When I heard yet another story about a fallen soldier, I felt a deep, vicarious grief for the family and for the remaining troops. Impotent rage welled up once again inside of me. Another family would now grieve the death of husband or wife, brother or sister, son or daughter. Another family would be changed forever.

Cathy and I were about to meet up for coffee at a small, tucked away Starbucks in our neighborhood. I arrived first and ordered my drink, already feeling on edge after driving behind a Hummer on my way to meet her. There was a rack of the daily newspapers near the area where I waited for my skinny vanilla latte. I had cancelled the daily newspaper at home because I was traumatized by the stories of war in Iraq. Now, glancing down at the *New York Times*, my gaze was met by a photo glaring back at me of a burned out vehicle in Baghdad, still smoking from the aftereffects of a blast, probably from an IED. Grabbing my coffee, I headed instinctively for the door. Cathy walked in just as I was about to burst out, hot tears were rolling unchecked down my face, my throat so raw with fresh grief I could barely speak. She grabbed both my arms and gazed into my eyes, mutely questioning what had just happened. I tried to tell her what I had just seen, and angry words, punctuated by expletives, came pouring from my mouth. We were standing to the side of the doorway as a middle-aged man squeezed through to get inside. Looking at us, he commiserated, "Aw, it can't be that bad, can it?" Cathy turned to him with a stern look and replied, "Oh, yes, it can be that bad!" before returning her attention to me and allowing me, nonjudgmentally, to continue on with my tirade.

I felt as though I couldn't go anywhere without being confronted by the ugliness of war, reminding me ever anew of the brutal death of my son. The "news" seemed to hiss at me from every direction, stirring up that scene forever nudging at the corners of my mind: not my mental picture of the explosion but the image of the two soldiers in dress uniform walking uninvited into our lives. That rewind played over and over. Day and night. Night and day. *Get out! Go back! Don't speak! Don't say those horrific words!*

I was angry as well over the unavoidable reality that my health, already precarious, was deteriorating. It was difficult at times to walk from my bedroom to the kitchen and living room. It was painful to perform simple tasks like grocery shopping, laundry, and meal preparation for our family. I understood that the emotional pain was exacerbating the physical and felt overwhelmed at the viciousness of this continuing cycle.

I missed my work with the students, work that would have constituted a welcome distraction from all that I was working through. The other two women who had lost their positions at church had secured new ones, but I wasn't looking for a job. I couldn't imagine the energy it would have taken to put together a résumé and take up a job search in the midst of grieving over David.

Wanting to try something new, something I had never done before, I thought I might have the energy to take a class—a goal of mine for my fiftieth year. It had to be something that wouldn't suck the remaining life out of me. I desired to be creative and artsy and to find at least a momentary distraction. Close to midnight on the day before my chosen class was to begin, I signed up for a watercolor painting class at a local community college.

I discovered to my surprised delight that I loved to paint, to play with colors on canvas. My flamboyant and eccentric instructor made the class fun and interesting, and I hoped I would be able through this avocation to escape to another place.

I not only found watercolor painting to be enjoyable and relaxing but reveled in my ability to do it anonymously. No one in my class knew about my story, or had to. For three hours on Monday afternoons I could escape to class and paint. My chosen distraction turned out to be lovely and therapeutic.

Jody joined me for the spring term class, and it was fun to bring a friend into my new world of painting. We could sit in class together and paint without having to speak. Jody was funny, continuously protesting her lack of an artistic bent, a self-criticism her work belied. To this day artistic expression has clearly become a part of her life, and it is both fun and satisfying for me to watch her flourish in class.

Aware of the depth of my wounds, Jody had early on declared that she wanted to remain nearby. The two of us continued to meet for prayer on Monday mornings, and she remained true to her self-proclaimed calling to function as a watchful friend—always on the lookout for signs of infection of any kind that might settle in and breed within me an increase in bitterness and despair. She spoke regularly to me of hope and healing.

At least for the moment, life was altered on Monday afternoons, as I worked with brushes and paint on paper. Even the messy paintings of a novice were soothing as I discovered the technique of mixing paints and water. Art was opening a new window of beauty and self-actualization, even if ever so slightly.

Then, as though to jar the weekly trajectory back to cruel reality, came Thursdays, and with each a concentrated hour of intense grief work. As Cindy helped me work through my labor of grief, we spent much of the time talking about my consuming emotion, anger. I was perpetually bottled up— tense, alarmed, skittish, and hyper-vigilant. I felt as though death could strike at any time and in any place. Reminiscent of the experience of the biblical Job, I fretted about the possibility of losing the rest of my family, of having them picked off one by one. Jesus "promises"—a warning without a maybe clause—in the Scriptures that in this world we *will* have trouble . . . following up with the assurance that He'll be with us in that time. He doesn't pledge that we'll be free from trouble, heartache, death, and tragedy, and this open-ended prospect never ceased to terrify me. I've known of other military moms who've lost more than one son or daughter. It could happen. *What if . . . ?*

My physical pain continued to worsen, to the point that it often hurt to drive, which led to isolation because I stayed home much of the time—as though the grief weren't isolating enough.

I was slowly emerging from the initial state of numbness, which meant that I was feeling increasingly the sadness and anger. Cindy and I talked about finding a release from my bottled up rage, and she suggested a myriad of techniques, from hitting my pillow to screaming into it to pounding Play-Doh to throwing plates. Wait! Hold on there, Cindy! Let's rewind. "Throwing *plates?!*" I asked, incredulous. She explained how she envisioned that very activity might look for me. "Have friends help you gather plates—cheap ones from a thrift store would work. Find a safe place where you'll do no harm and can clean up afterward. Throw those plates against a wall as hard as you can." Unaccountably— going against my grain as this did—I was excited about the plan. Who doesn't want to throw a plate without worrying about the consequence?

It's at this unlikely point that my dear friend Shelley enters my story in a significant way. Shelley is the epitome of a "safe" friend. We can say anything to each other and know there will be no judgment—just a lot of love and respect between us. Shelley had been on the high school staff for the youth group when I had worked in youth ministry. She was a rock star of a volunteer, as well. Students loved her. Staff loved her. I loved her.

At the time Shelley was working as a middle school teacher near my home. The school year had recently drawn to a close, and she was tying up loose ends in her classroom.

Knowing that an outside wall at her middle school had been slated for repainting over the summer, she asked her principal whether we could throw plates at it, to which he agreed. Some of Shelley's fellow teachers helped her find inexpensive plates, and a total of seventy were collected. This sounding like good therapy, some of these teachers told Shelley that they, too, wanted to throw plates at some point.

When I arrived at Shelley's classroom late in the afternoon she was ready to go, equipped with a rolling cart packed with seventy plates, a tarp, a broom and dust pan, folding chairs, and sharpies.

Shelley pushed her cart full of these essentials through her building, then outside to the wall of the gym, and went to work immediately. She laid the tarp out by the wall, unfolded the chairs, handed me a sharpie, and invited, "You may want to write down on the plates things you're angry at." We both sensed some tension, not to mention awkwardness at the prospect of exposing my raw anger and hurt in this unorthodox manner.

Having gone to a thrift shop earlier that day and purchasing three additional items that would uniquely represent the focus of my anger, I added them to the stacks of dishes that soon would be shards of glass and pottery, after first showing them to her.

The first was a glass vase, representing in my mind all the cut flowers delivered to our home after David's death. When we had first received them they were absolutely beautiful, and I was touched deeply by this thoughtful gesture—failing to anticipate my own response once the flowers all started to wilt and die. Cathy recalls my highly adverse reaction. Our home was filled with flowers and plants, so much so that there wasn't an empty space for any additional flower-filled vases. She asked a mutual friend who is a florist to come by and take care of the wilting and dead flowers and to rework the arrangements as needed, we being away from the house at the time. I didn't even know our florist friend was going to come over and work her magic, but when we arrived home the arrangements looked gorgeous and alive!

My friend had been there to help soothe my angst over the dying flowers, for which I had been grateful. I resolved that whenever I sent flowers in the future I would make sure, if at all possible, that the gift was a live plant. Now the glass vase represented the dead and wilted flowers that had undone me during those first few weeks.

The next item was a mug depicting a military theme. I have nothing against our military per se, the problem beings what the mug represented: war.

The last object of my ire that morning was a matching cup and saucer—fine china, decorated with dainty pink flowers. As soon as I saw it I knew what it represented: all of the religious platitudes and churchy clichés that had been directed my way. Words had been voiced that expressed a discomfort with ongoing grief and a desire for me to move on because, after all, my David was in heaven now. It was as though these glib words could simply wrap up everything for me and add to the package a nice, neat little bow.

I chose to fling the cup and saucer first, and the awkwardness started to fade as soon as the cup shattered against the high stucco wall. As I watched it break into a million tiny pieces the power of all of those misspoken words fell to the ground with them. Then I threw the vase, finding to my surprise that this piece was thick and more difficult to shatter, requiring a couple of tries. It was important to me to break it into small pieces, but the item proved stubborn. That accomplished, I started on the dishes, hurling one after another against the unsuspecting wall. With each revolution Shelley quietly handed me the sharpie, and I wrote on one plate after another about war, violence, pain, and suffering. I wrote the names of the men who had started the war and now didn't seem to know how to reverse the tide, how to wrap it up and bring our troops back home.

I kept throwing plates, drawing the alarmed attention of a school custodian who ventured outside and peered around the corner just as I was hurling another missive. He looked more than a little frightened at the sight of two obviously angry women and the broken shards of dishes littering the ground. Shelley gave him the okay signal, letting him know he needn't worry; this was business—if not official, then at least planned and sanctioned. Poor guy . . . he looked utterly bewildered.

I turned to Shelley and urged her to join me if she felt so inclined. I knew there were a couple of unresolved issues about which she might like to express her anger, too. Not requiring a second invitation, my friend jotted down some words and tossed a few plates while I rested my aching arms. By the time I had finished hurling the seventieth plate, a real element of catharsis had suffused me. The symbolic gesture hadn't remedied all of the issues, of course, but it had felt good to scream it out like a discus thrower before releasing the plates—even if I was screaming only in my head, it feeling too overwhelming to do so in front of Shelley.

It felt good to see those unfortunate plates shatter into tiny pieces.

It felt good to be honest about the intensity of my feelings.

Shelley then offered me a beautiful gift: she directed me to one of the folding chairs so I could rest. She sat with me for a while before picking up the push broom and dustpan and going to work. My friend singlehandedly cleaned up the entire mess—every shred of broken glass, china, and pottery, working quietly and brushing off my offers to help her. There was no hint of judgment or criticism from my friend. She loved me well and trusted the Lord to give me the continued strength to work through my grief.

Shelley dumped the last of the broken mess into a garbage can, and we started to talk about the ritual that had just taken place. We chuckled more than a little about how awkward it had felt to start out. There could have been no doubt I was uncomfortable to be that vulnerable with a friend. But the discomfort had dissipated fairly quickly, based on my knowledge of what a dear friend she was. I also knew that through the years she had trusted me with many of her own heart issues and that we were safe with each other. I had no reason to feel shame in the presence of my friend—who had at the same time, as well as on earlier occasions, been equally as vulnerable with me. I was proud of us and of our resourcefulness that day we flung plates against an outside wall of an elementary school. We had opted against keeping our pain bottled up, pretending it didn't exist. We had faced our hurt and confusion head on— had been honest and brave. We were warriors against the destruction of suffering and death. I was on my way to finding my voice, toward declaring the authenticity of my grief.

In the face of profound loss, I knew in my heart that I belonged to God and that He would never let me go. He was already then in the process of mending my shattered heart. Far from condemning me for expressing my grief and anger, He was surrounding me all the while with His grace, mercy, and lovingkindness.

The grace He gave me that day was a wide open space, on the cusp of which I stood poised to take my first halting steps in the direction of finding a new voice. Was the act of throwing plates another expression of lament? I wasn't sure, though I was trying on this approach, like a new pair of shoes, wondering what the walk of lament in all of its expressions would end up looking like in my life.

# Chapter 12

# To Comfort

Along with some of the letters we received came handmade quilts and blankets, sent to comfort our family from those across the country, unknown to us, who still saw us and desired to acknowledge our loss. Quilts fashioned with tender hands, boxed and delivered to our door. I imagined the circles of women gathered around to contribute their stitches, to place each square and to remember—and perhaps to pray. As each box was opened an overwhelming sense of David's loss would in turn open the floodgates. I would put the box away, resolved to look at its contents another day. Thinking about the other mothers across the nation receiving quilts, I wondered whether they too stored away the kind gifts or whether they opted to display or use them.

One day a box arrived with yet another quilt, quite unlike any other. It was the identity of the quilt maker, as well as her lovely letter, that touched me deeply. Had I not caught sight of the letter, the significance of the gift and its creator—the gift of her love—might well have been passed over.

This contribution wasn't from a stranger; the letter was from a young woman who had been in the same church youth group as David. She spoke of being shy and quiet—not one of the popular girls, not one who would have been remembered. She remembered David, however, and recalled specific characteristics about him that had developed within her an increasing respect for him. She remembered his smile, his laughter, and his kindness. She wrote of her respect for his willingness to courageously serve our country, . . . and of her sorrow upon learning of his death. She reported that she now flies her American flag on significant holidays and anniversaries, specifically in remembrance of David.

She went on to share her story of the making of the quilt and how it had taken longer than usual because she was the only one working on it and put in long shifts as a nurse in a large Portland area hospital. Each stitch, she recounted, carried a prayer for us, David's family. Tears had often accompanied the prayers as she had woven together the pieces of the fabric to form a lovely quilt to memorialize a young boy who alone had befriended her and showed her kindness. Hers was a thoughtful gift, a sacrifice of love. Later, when our grandchildren were babies, I would remove it from the linen closet and lay it on the floor for the babies to lie on. The quilt afforded them an extra layer of warmth and comfort as they learned to roll from side to side.

I received a call from the Oregon representative of the Home of the Brave Quilt Project, Kaye Vicars Hansen. The organization is a nationwide group that has carried the history of quilt making from the 1800s through to the present day. Kaye explained that she had a gift to present to us and asked us to set a date on which she could come to our home and present us with a quilt handmade by several individuals in Oregon. She briefly told me about a group calling themselves the Oregon State Quilters who sewed replicas of The Cross X or Album Quilt, a reproduction of the US Sanitary Commission Quilts. She would share more information when she arrived for the presentation.

Upon her arrival I learned about the history of quilt making in the United States to memorialize loved ones lost in war, national tragedies, and significant political movements. I learned that these quilts had been fashioned since 1826 to demonstrate the love and support of the quilters themselves, as well as to express their political persuasions. She presented us also with an official document about our quilt, which reads as follows:

*Home of the Brave Quilt Project*
*Staff Sgt. David J R Weisenburg, Army National Guard*
*September 13, 2004 near Camp Taji, Iraq*
—A Brief History of the Civil War Soldier's Quilts

During the U.S. Civil War, a volunteer organization called the U.S. Sanitary Commission was formed with the purpose of raising supplies and funds for the North and of overseeing the sanitary conditions of military hospitals. From this Commission, many significant Americans, including Clara Barton, Dorthea Dix and Frederick Law

Olmstead, went on to achieve greatness by beginning America's social and medical movements. A general call went out in 1860 for the donations of quilts and coverlets for the soldiers' use.

The U.S. Sanitary Commission requested that quilts measure 48 by 84 inches, as these quilts were given to soldiers to carry as part of their bedrolls and were used in military hospitals on wounded soldiers' cots. In 2 ½ years the Women's Auxiliary made and donated to the Union troops over 250,000 quilts. Of these quilts only 5 are known to exist today; primarily because of the wear and tear of use during the military campaigns and also because soldiers were often buried with their quilts. Only one of these quilts is in the public domain and it is on display at the Lincoln Memorial Shrine in Redlands, California. It is a national treasure.

Because of the shortage of finished textiles in the confederacy, Southern women gave Confederate troops priceless family heirloom quilts. Quilts that they made were often from homespun cloth and used newspapers as lining to provide warmth. Southern women also contributed to fund raising events by raffling quilts to raise funds to buy Confederate gunboats. These quilts were often raffled more than once and the women who made them were affectionately known as "Gunboat Ladies."

*Just as the women of the Civil War honored the brave soldiers who fought on both sides, the Oregon State Quilters have made this replica of a Civil*

*War Soldier's Quilt as an expression of our deepest appreciation of the service and sacrifice made by the United States brave service personnel in the Iraq and Afghanistan conflicts.*

—Don Beld Kaye Vicars Hansen

National Coordinator Oregon State Coordinator

Holding in my arms now the replica of a Civil War blanket, a piece of history, I was struck by the depth of meaning in our receiving this particular quilt. There were more profound messages still, handwritten on the fabric. Kaye had sent squares of fabric to my friend Renee, asking her to pass them along to our closest friends, each of whom was instructed to write on her square a brief message and to sign her name. Renee then gathered the squares, etched with love, and mailed them back to Kaye. As I look upon the quilt and catch sight of the names of friends and family we hold dear, I am literally touched by their love and friendship. As I wrap the quilt around myself in the rocking chair, the arms of friends enwrap and hold me near. They gather my tears and hold me close—a tangible gift.

Another blanket sent to warm and comfort arrived from Pendleton Woolen Mills here in Oregon, a generous gift given with a kind word sewn into the wool:

*"Grateful Nation Honoring those who serve our country in the Armed Forces"*

—Pendleton Woolen Mills

Who are these kind men and women, these agents of comfort and kind support? They quietly bestow gifts and speak prayers over the grieving throughout the country, anonymously and for no personal acclaim. We are grateful to be so kindly acknowledged by them, and it is my hope that at least some one of them will in turn receive my acknowledgment recorded here.

Another gift, a crown jewel from the hands of a craftsman, is offered to the Oregon families of the fallen in Iraq and Afghanistan. A Southern Oregon woodworker sharing his sorrow on our behalf has constructed mahogany chests, engraved with the flag the deceased once carried, in memory of those we have loved and lost.

As the families gathered for this presentation, we found comfort in the newly forged bond that links us, former strangers who now share the deepest level of brotherhood and sisterhood, and in the weaving of stories reverently spoken in the parking lot of a local mall in Portland by those assembled on the basis of one man's attempt to work out his personal pain, forging from it gifts of exquisite beauty. We lingered a little longer, overcome by a sense that we were standing on holy ground, acknowledging that we had shared sacred stories.

The owner of a Willamette Valley winery, sensing the sanctity of the occasion, extended an invitation to the Oregon families of the fallen to attend a private dinner at his establishment. It was a time for conversation, of connecting, and of holding. Our families gathered with no agenda, no ceremony, and no camera to capture still-life glimpses of the tear-filled eyes. Who knew that we had needed this gathering? We hadn't realized it ourselves, though the occasion established a bond of love and shared experience among families who have lost in a war. As Jim and I made the drive home from the wine country of Oregon, we spoke of our gratefulness to those in our community, strangers we had never before met, who cared so deeply and had touched our hearts in ways we could never have expected.

Though my heart sings a lament, there is a weaving of gratitude in the singing, a song of quiet kindnesses beyond imagination.

Another gift arrives, this one in pencil etched on paper, a drawing framed and signed. A drawing of David's face on the day he arrived home on leave for his sister's wedding. The artist captures his smile, his joy at being home, and his anticipation of the ceremony to take place on the following day. It took me eleven years to finally hang the illustration of David in our hallway, along with his awards and commendations. Not far from the portrait, sitting on a small table, sits the wooden figure of a mother holding the folded American flag to her chest.

"*Oh God of Comfort and Father of mercies, your fingerprint, your touch is all over this story with the song of comfort given, sung by the unknown. I held it at arm's length, so overwrought with pain I couldn't take it all in when it was given. My anger, my pain filled my heart, and the shroud of grief hung bitterly 'round. Your grace-song over me is greater; greater than my pain, and I am washed in your compassionate mercy anew.*"

*Chapter 13*

# Anniversaries

S andwiched between Jason's reception and Daniel's wedding was the month of May, a month through which I struggled for various reasons. David's birthday marked its beginning. How could we navigate the day of his birth after his departure from our midst? Less than two weeks beyond that hurdle would fall Mother's Day, and a few days after that my birthday. Topping it all off would be Memorial Day, the day on which we recognize all of the military personnel no longer in our midst. In all honesty, still today I'd rather skip the month of May. In conversations with other mothers of fallen soldiers I find ready agreement. Despite its inherent loveliness and seasonal promise, May can be a tough month to navigate.

The first time we faced David's birthday, bereft, we woke up early, intending to tackle some gardening. Our home had been constructed only the year before, and landscaping was an ongoing venture. We had a large, mostly empty lot, and it was begging for more trees, bushes, and flowers.

After David's death we were gifted with several trees in his memory, including memorial varieties—boxwood, a flowering cherry, and a Japanese maple—from all of our kids' in-laws. Jody and Rhonda contributed a magnolia to plant out by the swing, and Barry and Denise planted another in our front yard where we could see and enjoy it from the dining room window.

When we moved into our home Clark and Cathy had given us our first new tree, a pink dogwood that still blooms every May. When I turned fifty my daughter invited my friends to a luncheon in her home to celebrate; one of them presented me with a rosebush to plant in our new yard. After we had planted our dogwood we positioned the rosebush near the huge oak tree already present in our front yard. At the same time we tied a large yellow ribbon around the majestic oak, a tradition for families of loved ones who are in the military serving in a war. At that time David was alive and serving in Iraq.

On May 2, 2005, David would have turned twenty-seven, and our family had planned to come over and help us do some gardening. We were up around 6:30 in the morning. Jim was in the study, sitting at his desk, and I joined him there. We sat there silent for a time before addressing the elephant in the room: *How do we do this? How do we get through this day—our precious son's anniversary of birth?*

Breathe—just breathe.

I vividly recalled the details of that birth, ten days prior to his due date. I remembered meeting the little one whom I had nearly delivered prior to my arrival at the hospital. I had been convinced I would be having another girl and was delighted to meet our first baby boy with his dark hair and eyes.

Without warning or preamble my mind's eye jumped, then, to that all too familiar image of the two men in dress uniform walking through our door. "*NO! Don't speak! Get out!*" I wanted to cry out. Trying to eradicate the recurring recollection, I leaned my head on Jim's shoulder and . . . noticed in my peripheral vision something red in our yard. Walking over to the window, my gaze took in a single red rose, resplendent under the oak tree. One red rose, in full bloom, at 6:30 in the morning in early May. That just doesn't happen. Shaking our heads, we made our way outside to see for ourselves. There, indeed, appeared a stunning red rose from the bush my friend had given me a year earlier in honor of my fiftieth birthday. Roses were especially significant to me in that they had been the flowers my David would regularly bring home to me. We looked at each other in wonder and disbelief. My Creator had touched me intimately with this blooming specimen. It was as though He were assuring me, "I see you and your pain, and I am with you."

The sadness was overwhelming and intense on that first Mother's Day without David. The pain of "celebrating" without all of my children present felt excruciating. A part of me was missing. I went through the motions, wishing I had stayed in bed and slept the day away, oblivious. But once again gravity prevailed. Remembering my surviving children and their need for their mom's presence, I turned my back on that temptation to check out. Over the years the impact of these significant days has gotten softer—less intense, though not necessarily easier. And the joy of holding grandchildren has opened my heart to a precious and unexpected iteration of the recurring gift of life.

The first anniversary of David's death was approaching. What would this day hold? I felt a sense of dread as we counted down on the calendar, remembering where we had been and what we'd been doing just one year earlier. Jim and I wanted to formulate some kind of plan for the day, though we struggled with what that might look like. The feelings of dread lessened at bit, however, after we had made some decisions.

We decided on three separate gatherings to mark the anniversary of David's passing. First, we would have an open house for his friends, all of whom we contacted, inviting our family, as well. This was a bittersweet occasion, replete with shared stories and memories, as well as much laughter. Marking this day together made it a significant time to honor a friend, a son, a brother. I arranged all of David's awards, medallions, pictures, ribbons, and flag on the buffet table so his friends would have an opportunity to view the display, keeping them up through the following evening for our second gathering.

For this occasion Jim and I invited our own close friends who had known David to share stories and memories of our son. It felt good and even empowering to hear his name spoken without reservation among us, as many of us still struggled through expressions of grief. Jim and I spoke honestly of our grief in this gathering of friends who loved and cared for us. It was a part of the healing process for us to hear and be heard.

Finally, we arranged to be together as a family on September 13. The newlyweds Daniel and Adina flew in from Nebraska to round out the circle. We had discussed in advance how we would like to spend the day.

It felt awkward. How would we as remaining family members navigate a day like this? We certainly couldn't go about it in a business-as-usual mode, as though it didn't hold in our hearts a reality so deeply poignant and significant. Everyone wanted to take the day off and travel as a group somewhere out of town. We opted for the beach. Our friends loaned us their Suburban for the day, it being spacious enough to accommodate our entire family.

Before heading out to the beach we drove to the cemetery and stood at David's grave together. There were some colorful flowers on his gravestone, as well as a note. We arranged the flowers we ourselves and brought and added fresh water to the green plastic vases provided by the cemetery. Elizabeth laid some flowers on Ben Isenberg's grave, as well. He had fittingly been buried right next to David.

As we stood there silently on the northeast hill at Willamette National Cemetery overlooking the city of Portland, I kept reminding myself to breathe. This place, and the marking of the anniversary, seemed overwhelming and surreal, representing our new normal as a family— though everything within me wanted to deny that this was happening to us. I didn't want my family to have to endure this horrendous grief for even one more day. How could we keep doing this year after year? I entertained magical thinking: *maybe David is on a covert mission and will rejoin us shortly! This can't be the end of his story here on earth. This can't be the end of our stories with him. I want more time with my son!* In a flash I saw in my mind's eye yet again our all-too-frequent visitors, those two soldiers in dress uniform walking solemnly and silently through our door, uninvited, invading the sanctity of our peaceful home.

I could hear Daniel clearing his throat, silently, tears rolling down his face, and I prayed that the Lord would strengthen and comfort our kids as they faced their own grief. We all shed silent tears at David's grave on that morning of September 13, 2005, struggling to find our collective voice. This was our reality. We were that family who had lost a son, a brother, and a brother-in-law in the war in Iraq, and I despised this new identity.

Filing into the Suburban, we continued on to Pacific City. It was quiet at first, and then, gradually, the usual Weisenburg conversations and banter picked up. When we reached Pacific City it was a little chilly outside—one of those typical Oregon beach days with the ever-present mist in the air. The younger generation decided to climb the sand dunes and run down them as fast as they could, just as they had done as children. Jim and I watched the dory boats as they quickly approached the shoreline, one after another. We delighted as well in observing the kids, now adults, playing with abandon on the dunes. We had lunch at the nearby pub before leaving to drive south to Lincoln City.

I was glad that this was my second trip to Lincoln City since David's death. Several months earlier Jim and I had made the excursion to the beach with our home group from church. At that time, as we drove through Lincoln City on the way to the house we had rented with our friends, I was overcome with emotion and couldn't stop sobbing. At first I was uncertain what had triggered my tears, but eventually I made the association with our spring and summer family weekends at the beach. A few times we had stopped here and gone shopping in several of the antique stores. David had always been the one who would accompany me on these antiquing jaunts, noticing and appreciating the details in which I delighted. As Jim and I drove past each store David and I had visited, successive waves of grief seemed to slap at me. The rest of that weekend was rough; I had been completely unprepared for the memories that rose like a threatening flood. Exhausted with grief, we had left our friends early on Sunday.

Now, once again in Lincoln City and with the memories intact, I was gratified to recognize that they didn't pull me down in the same way they had months earlier. I was grateful to be present with our family.

To the surprise and delight of all, Jim and I devised and followed through on a silly plan. We drove to the nearby casino, handed each family member ten dollars, and advised them that they had twenty minutes to try to be the highest roller among the eight of us. We laughed when most of them came back before ten minutes was up; it doesn't take long to blow through ten dollars in a casino, and nearly all returned empty-handed. When Elizabeth rejoined us, however, it was with the distinct honor of being the only winner. She decided to take her meager winnings and treat us to ice cream.

Later on we went out for pizza before making our way back home. Throughout the day we engaged in conversation about David, noting how he would have loved this day of playfulness. At the pizza parlor the kids found the game room and went a little crazy. The pent-up anxiety that had led up to the day had come spilling out throughout its course: the running down the sand dunes in Pacific City, tearing around the casino, savoring ice cream before dinner, and now challenging one another to video games. One of our number found a machine that offered rubber balls, each with a long and springy rubber band attached to it. Everyone bought one.

On the way home in the Suburban the rubber ball boomerangs were all over the place, appearing as though out of nowhere in the dark. Everyone was grabbing at them, trying to collect them all. Jason, attempting to concentrate on driving, was irritated with the rest of us, directing us in his best tough-guy Marine voice to settle down. It was apparent that Cindy, seated up front commiserating with him, had all she could do to keep from laughing. The uproarious hilarity did us all good, and we each acknowledged in satisfaction that David would have loved every moment. He would have been as exasperated as Jason on our drive home, yes, and he probably would have been surprised about our trip to the casino.

We were to discover the serendipity of several unexpected days of remembrance throughout the year, the succession of which would contribute to our new normal. I'm not altogether certain we've made the adjustment even now.

It is common for those who have lost a loved one to commemorate the day of their birth, that of their death, and all the significant holidays associated with the person's memory. Anyone who has lost a close family member knows exactly how fraught those holidays can be with pain and the missing of the loved one. I have experienced this as well following the deaths of both of my parents and of my older sister. What I didn't anticipate, however, was the powerful hold that national holidays such as Memorial Day, Flag Day, the Fourth of July, and Veterans' Day would have on me. Like dots on a page to be connected by pencil lines, these successive commemorations constituted yet another new landscape through which to navigate.

Thanksgiving is a time when family members traditionally gather for a shared banquet, yet when one is missing the thought of preparing, let alone sharing a festive feast can be grueling. I am convinced to begin with that the sentimental commercials and television movies depicting the ideal American family posed, smiling, around am impeccably set table portray a sentimentalized reality quite unlike that of most of the people I know. I'll call this the

Disneyland holiday—the one to which we all aspire, and the one we naively, year after year, continue to expect.

As soon as Thanksgiving is over, the Christmas season hits hard, its foot already on the accelerator. Rampant commercialism/consumerism is at its peak, and no matter what our frame of mind at any given moment we can't avoid the sappy holiday music assaulting our ears at every turn. It has been my practice for years to prepare far enough ahead of time to avoid the glitz and glitter that have nothing whatever to do with the birth of Jesus.

I typically can't avoid the last-minute grocery shopping, however. It seems that, every December since David was killed, every time I set foot in a grocery store I'm met with the schmaltzy promise that "I'll Be Home for Christmas" and find myself standing in the middle of the produce department tearing up. I just wanted some salad fixings, but the lyrics of this tune never fail to strike a deep cord in me. No, I remind myself, my David *isn't* coming home, this Christmas or at any other time, . . . *so would you please quit blasting these songs in the grocery store?* I have heard other moms who have lost children recount a similar story and share like feelings. It has been consoling to discover that I'm not alone in carrying such sad feelings at that time of year touted everywhere, against the tide of obvious reality, as idyllic and magical.

Envisioning our family spending the upcoming Christmas for a second time without David's presence seemed initially too much to bear. David, who had relished the entire season, would have inaugurated the extended holiday as soon as the eggnog appeared on the grocery shelf. When he enlisted in the Army right out of high school, I was realistic enough to realize that he would spend a few Christmases away from family. Yet our son had found a way to make it home every single Christmas—even when stationed in South Korea for a year. The first Christmas after his death, then, was in contrast all the more painful.

With the second Christmas approaching, the shock and numbness were wearing off, though the idea of another holiday season without this cherished family member filled my heart with such poignant sadness as to nearly immobilize me. One evening in early December a friend dropped by to say hello just as Jim and I were about to leave for a meeting. We had set up our large, pre-lit artificial tree a few days before, feeling that this nod to the holiday was all we could manage. My friend, an interior designer by profession, noticed immediately that our Christmas tree had nothing but lights on it and inquired about my plans to decorate, as the boxes of ornaments were setting nearby. I replied honestly that I was stuck and really didn't care, and she, knowing that we were about to leave, asked our permission to stay and decorate our tree. Aware that she was a busy lady and that others paid her to decorate their homes for Christmas, I was taken aback by her generous offer. I readily agreed, however, and we returned home later in the evening to a beautifully bedecked tree. Such kindness!

The reality of David's death was slowly beginning to settle in, although I reverted to a stage of deep denial every time those fleeting visions of his being on a covert mission entered my head. As we neared that second Christmas without him, though—that year when I was stuck and couldn't decorate the tree—I cried quiet tears of acknowledgment as I put out everyone's stockings by the fireplace, again including David's. Because I knew full well he wouldn't be joining us.

I have learned that conversation surrounding another "anniversary" of sorts remains painful to Elizabeth. On August 14, 2004, my daughter married Erik; this was a day marked by joy and celebration as these two united their hearts. It is indeed Elizabeth and Erik's anniversary, but it is also the last day our family was together in one place.

The family portrait taken on that day takes pride of place in our living room—a bittersweet marker and milestone. Too often, however, when I have spoken of the picture, especially in Elizabeth's presence, I have described it as the last picture taken of our family rather than as the family photo taken at our daughter's wedding. The portrait and its meaning have threatened to eclipse the observance of her day, and when she alluded to me of her associated pain I was saddened by my unintentional callousness and apologized for the pain I had inflicted. To this day I take pains to be mindful of the manner in which I speak of her day.

The anniversaries of our last complete family gathering and of David's death have indeed overshadowed both Elizabeth's anniversary and her birthday, which we had celebrated only three days before David was killed. The aromas of death and loss intertwine around our celebrations of those days, seeping into our lives and tingeing joy with sorrow.

As Elizabeth's birthday approaches every year, it is my hope that she will recognize anew how deeply loved and cherished she is, that she may know in the midst of her own sadness that she has not become a casualty, discarded to some degree, however subtle, in the dust surrounding her brother's memory. He it is who has been called a fallen American hero. But it is imperative for me as a mother to not lose touch of the feelings and sensitivities of the surviving family members.

There was yet another hurdle to jump, one we didn't see coming for a while. Jason and Daniel, our twins, were twenty-three years of age when David was killed—his younger brothers. When they were approaching their twenty-seventh birthdays, both suffered quiet agony in anticipation of the upcoming celebration. Daniel and Adina were by that point living in Portland, and we planned to celebrate the twins' joint birthday together for the first time in several years. Each of them, however, privately communicated to us their preference not to do so. In each instance I gently probed, only to learn that neither had ever imagined passing their older brother in age. Without having communicated their angst to one another, each was overwhelmed by the new layer of grief they were experiencing. Jim and I felt it best to let them work through their pain individually, but once again I observed in my mind's eye those two soldiers in dress uniform walking through our door—and once again I screamed at them to get out. My imperative never changes the story, which invariably unfolds in the same way. I hate the way my children have been torn apart, deeply and terribly wounded by the brutal death of their brother. I want to change the storyline for their sakes, but it is beyond my power to do so. I have to let them wrestle with the issues, even as I do. I must release them, must resist trying to get in the way of the unfolding of their personal grief processes.

On Jason and Daniel's twenty-seventh birthday they agreed to a quiet family dinner. I thought them both courageous to agree to celebrate their birth and the marking of this pivotal year in our family's saga. I am gratified to report that I stepped into the day not with pain and sorrow but with joy at yet another commemoration of the births of my twin sons—the sons I cherish so deeply.

I find myself able to inhale deeply, breathing in His grace. As we continue to celebrate anniversaries, birthdays, and holidays, I acknowledge and hold closely to the realization that His grace is infinitely greater than my pain and grief.

# Chapter 14

# Grace

When we were young my younger sister, Julie, and I rummaged through a closet in our parents' bedroom. We knew there were pictures and mementos our parents had stored away, and we would often look through them, hoping to discover something new. We loved looking at the pictures of our parents and their early years in Huron, South Dakota, with our older sister and brother. Their lives had been so different from those we had experienced living in Portland, Oregon. At this point we were not aware that there had been another sibling besides Nancy and Ronnie. There was one box we had never opened, though we were curious about what it might contain. It had been placed by itself in the right hand corner of highest closet shelf. One day we did reach it, lifting it up and carrying it to our parents' bed, where we peered inside together. What we discovered was a long pink ribbon bearing a name in satin letters: Barbara Ann. Digging further, we found some black and white photos of a tiny baby, labeled as having been born in April 1942. Some of the pictures showed her, as though on display, asleep in a tiny white box.

Mystery surrounded this little one. Who was she? What had happened to her? Where was she now? We made our way to the kitchen, where our mom was baking bread, and solemnly asked her about this Barbara Ann. Our mother simply explained that she was our older sister, Barbara, calling her a "blue baby." Our sister, she went on, had been born with a heart defect and had died on the day after her birth. From our wondering perspective our mother seemed stoic, matter-of-fact, disconnected in the way she responded. That was to my recollection the extent of the conversation.

I recall no tears gathering in her eyes as she continued to knead the dough on the wooden breadboard in our kitchen. We wondered, though, about baby Barbara—what it would have been like to grow up with another older sister. Barbara had entered the world twelve years before my own birth. We looked at the pictures a while longer, eventually placing everything carefully back inside the box and moving on.

We traded bedrooms with our parents at some point during our elementary years, and from my bed I looked up at the plaque my parents had hung on the wall containing the words of Isaiah 30:15: "In repentance and rest you shall be saved, in quietness and trust is your strength." As a child I had no idea what this meant or why my parents had seen fit to hang it there. I would think about it, however, and wish I knew what God was trying to communicate to me.

I would also look up periodically at the top far end of the closet, if the door wasn't shut all the way. I could see the box still residing there, containing those meager mementos of my sister, Barbara. I imagined again what it would be like to have another older sister, closer to my own age, and imagined a friendship with her as we grew up together. I found to my mild surprise and confusion that I missed her presence in my life without even having known her.

I was saddened for my mother, with her baby passing away soon after her birth, and wished there were more to her story. I wondered why my parents had always said they had four children, when in reality there had been five. I was feeling a child's grief for my sister, though I had no idea how to express it. It comforted me to learn about my Uncle Bobbie, who still lived in South Dakota, and how he remembered and honored her life. My uncle, who was kind and attentive, would place flowers on Barbara's grave every year on her birthday and on Christmas. I was glad to know she had not been forgotten.

One year when Julie and I were adults we traveled back to South Dakota for a family reunion, taking our husbands to the family farm that had been established in 1916 and where our cousin now lives. Not far from the homestead is the cemetery where several family members were buried. We decided we would try to find Barbara Ann's grave. It took a while, but we finally located her marker near our grandparents' graves. Although I didn't speak out loud, I thought through the words I wanted to speak to her: that I was sorry she had died so young and that I promised to remember her and the date of her birth. I wanted to understand why she was only rarely spoken of in our family.

Some years later I visited Barbara's grave again, bringing five pink roses intermingled with baby's breath, held together by a long pink satin ribbon. I laid them on my sister's grave, assuring her that I would not forget there had been five of us and that I looked forward to meeting her one day.

One November, when I was attending the Northwest Women's Prayer Summit, I met a woman named Grace. It had been just over a year since David had been killed, and I estimated her age to be about seventy or a little older; she was a petite woman whose feet barely touched the floor when she sat in our circle. As we shared a meal together I listened to part of her story. Although she was spry, she wasn't well. She and her husband had raised three children, one son and two daughters. A short time earlier Grace and her husband had buried their only son, who had died from complications of AIDS. We wept together as we shared details about the deaths of our sons, commiserating with one another about how utterly devastating it is to lose a child. Our hearts began to knit together over our shared losses.

There was a part of me that hadn't wanted to attend the Prayer Summit that year. Preoccupied by my angry feelings over David's death, the ongoing war in Iraq, my poor health, and my job loss, I had feared that rancor over my own issues would spill over and poison the other women with whom I spoke. I also worried about the possibility of hearing more platitudes like "God has a plan" or "Just trust Him" or "David's in heaven now." My defenses were up. I couldn't pray . . . so why was I there to begin with? I feared that, if provoked, I might explode in anger—or worse. Thankfully, what I experienced was quite the opposite of the responses I had feared: grace, empathetic sorrow, and the room to express my grief.

I did, however, experience one uncomfortable conversation in the dining room toward the end of the week. I was reacquainting with a woman, a friend of a friend, who was visibly sorry to hear about David's death and expressed her inability to imagine how I must be feeling. It was comforting to hear her say those words, but as we continued dialoguing she seemed agitated, divulging that she struggled to reconcile what she was learning at church with what she believed to be true. She had always been convinced that *God doesn't give us more than what we can handle*. While wanting to avoid conflict with this woman or starting an argument, I strongly disagreed with her taking a verse referring to sin and temptation out of context. I believe that the troubles and challenges of life *are* so much more than we can handle that we sorely need a Savior to help us negotiate them. We need Jesus—need to lean in to Him, our solid rock, not only in times of trouble but in all times.

I spoke to her pointedly, in an emphatic tone I knew to be less than charitable, about atrocities like the Holocaust, the genocide in Rwanda, and the tsunami that had only recently taken more than 280,000 lives. I spoke about all of the families, including my own, that had lost a loved one in a war. These stories of loss, she had to agree, were completely over the top and too much for any one individual to "handle." There was an awkward silence and some shed tears on both sides of the conversation. I emphasized that it is precisely in those times when I am completely and utterly devastated with sorrow and grief, when my pain and loss are indeed *too much*, that all I can do is fall at the feet of Christ and pray for His boundless grace to carry me, to remind me that He is there, . . . *because I can't handle my son's brutal, violent death, and I need my Savior.*

Later, in my room, I found myself rattled by that conversation in the dining room. I felt angry about Scripture having been misused and taken out of context, . . . but mostly about having hurt this well-meaning individual by my vehement comments, which I suspected had come off as caustic. I had hoped that this week of prayer would constitute for me an oasis time in which I would find mercy and rest for my aching soul—not a time of shame over the way I was handling my grief. I wanted not to "Christianize" but to speak hope and hear it spoken.

I considered skipping the next meeting time—an impulse similar to the all-too-common desire to retreat back home; crawl, defeated, into my own bed; and stay there for a while. I was exhausted. My roommate was getting ready to walk over to the meeting, however, and I decided to resist these inclinations and accompany her. After all, it was to be the last meeting of the day. I went but did so reluctantly, feeling angry, annoyed, and hurt.

When I entered the meeting room with its seventy or so chairs set up in a circle, I noticed the low table with candles and beautiful draped golden fabrics, along with exquisitely carved crosses and the communion elements of bread and grape juice on the table. After a time of worship and prayer lasting for more than an hour, we were instructed to serve one another communion. We were instructed to quietly pray, asking the Lord to direct us to the person we were to serve.

I sat there with my eyes closed, not thinking clearly enough to pray for God's direction. It had been difficult for me to join in the spirit of this time of worship and prayer. I kept mulling over the conversation I'd had earlier in the dining room, thinking of other things I could have said. I felt my heart soften as I remembered, once again, how deeply the grace of God had touched me, and I began to pray about extending that grace to my friend in the dining room.

The lights were dimmed, and I heard movement around me. Women were beginning to serve other women the cup and the bread. I thought about Grace and our connection, having both lost sons. I thought about how tiny and frail she seemed, . . . and yet she had exuded grace to me. How aptly named she was! I believed it was Grace to whom I would serve communion. But when I was about to stand and walk over to the table to pick up a cup of juice and tear off a piece of the bread, I felt someone close. I opened my eyes, and there she was, kneeling before me, looking up at me with a strong intention to extend love and mercy. Grace. Petite and frail Grace.

Kneeling before me! Before the angry, prideful, and self-righteous me. I whispered, "I should be serving you,

Grace!" She softly and firmly declined, insisting that she would be serving me. She did so with a prayer of comfort, healing, and hope over me. I started once again to feel ashamed of my angry outburst directed at the well-meaning woman with whom I had spoken earlier, but the shame washed off me as she continued to pray. I was overcome by the forgiveness and the grace of God pouring from Grace's lips. After praying, Grace stood up and held me close.

I remember thinking about how desperately I needed Jesus. As I drove home the next day I thought about how much I need Jesus for every step I take as I walk this journey of grief and lament. I could so easily become entangled with words misspoken, so easily go off on a tangent. I thought about how grateful I was for the grace of God poured out on me. I wanted to be an extension of His grace to those around me, too—like the woman with whom I had spoken in the dining room, and to those who have made hurtful comments or tried to tell me to stop crying because "David's in heaven now."

I thought a lot during the ensuing week, as I watched the waves of the Pacific Ocean crash against the shore, about my counselor's observation that grief is like the ebb and flow of the ocean. I thought about God's love washing over me as I grieved and lamented my David. As the waves crashed in the cold November surf, I wondered how long this horrific grief would continue to weigh me down. Part of me wanted to go out with the surf and not come back. I was weary of weeping and missing that which his death had wrested from our family.

Would God's grace be enough to heal my broken heart?

I thought about a verse, Hebrews 13:5, someone had read aloud during the week about His promise to never leave or forsake me. I thought about Grace and about how willing and courageous she had been to share her own story of grief over a lost son. And I thought about what I had learned from her and how we would remember our sons together. Then I remembered my own mother and her time of sorrow, and, oh, how I wished a woman like Grace had been able to reach out to her after the death of her Barbara Ann. How different her ongoing story might have been.

God showed up in my story at the prayer summit. He broke through to me with His love and grace. As I gazed out at Haystack Rock in Cannon Beach, I remembered something a friend had said to me years earlier about God being the rock and refuge that can never erode. He who is always strong will in turn strengthen me, will be the ever solicitous Shepherd who carries me, even when I feel as though I can't take another step forward on this long and painful journey. He doesn't reject me even when I feel so angry I could easily break seventy more plates, . . . and then another seventy.

*Chapter 15*

# Fog

A thick blanket of wintry fog settled in on Portland's Mount Scott. It was mid-January, 2006, when we returned from the trip of a lifetime in Maui with our adult children and their spouses, followed by another week there with dear friends. We basked in the warm tropical sun, thoroughly enjoying the "spirit of aloha" and the company of those with whom we vacationed. I was tanned and rested after a literal oasis time from the trappings of the grief that still clung to my home and my heart.

It was Monday morning, and soon Jody and Rhonda would arrive for our regular prayer time for our families. We continued to meet on Monday mornings for years after David died and their sons returned from their deployments to Iraq. As I looked out my living room window, from which vantage point I had once gazed at that rainstorm within a rainstorm after David's death, I observed the fog wrapping itself around the tall evergreens in my neighborhood. There was an unexplainable beauty and mystery in the picture. My heart resonated with the heavy fog, whose tendrils seemed once again to be wrapping themselves around my heart and mind, threatening to obliterate me, drag me under, and hold me there. The tension was real; the gravity of death was vying for my full attention, though the upward impetus of life and redemption stories was starting to gain momentum.

Would I continue to do my grief work? To face the reality of David's death? Would the God-given courage to move forward continue to flow through me? I knew the drill: one step at a time. Would my anger shift, clearing the path for my feet? The longer I stared out the window at the fog, the more I felt an inner exhaustion setting in as I contemplated the grief work ahead of me. I wondered whether this intensity would ever dissipate. My tears were ever present, and I wasn't ashamed of them; they were a part of meeting my grief with honesty. Jesus wept, so who was I to deny the pain and sorrow that filled my heart?

Jody walked in from the fog and sat down with me in my living room. Rhonda was away celebrating her birthday, so it would be just the two of us meeting today. I spoke with Jody about the inner fog that threatened to keep me from the grief work ahead of me, admitting how easy it would be to lean in to a place thick with confusion, to choose a road that seemed easier rather than a place of clarity, honesty, and truth . . . along with facing this horrific pain.

Jody spoke of the possibility of a clearing of the fog that was keeping me from seeing the places where God wanted to show up and break through my story. Grief had been weighing me down to such an extent that it was a challenge to remember those places of His mercy, to intentionally walk into the light; instead, the fog of grief would roll in, perniciously wrapping its fingers around my heart and constricting it still further, so that I would almost forget where and when it was the Lord had shown up. I would fail to think about His mercy and the intimate ways in which He had and would continue to reveal His love for me.

Jody reminded me the watercolor class we had taken together a year earlier and asked whether I was working on anything at that time. I told her that I had painted a picture of a lamenter bowed down in the dark, a depiction of the aloneness I felt as I cried out to the Lord in my sorrow and pain, despite the perception that my prayers were bouncing off the ceiling; I shared with her my seeming inability to connect with Him in the way I once had.

She began to rehearse back to me my own shared memories of those times the Lord had indeed broken through my story with His mercy and grace, had met with me in the unexpected ways. "Marilyn, remember the red rose that bloomed on David's birthday? And remember the dance of the hummingbird right in front of you and Elizabeth when you were sitting together on the deck last spring? Remember the rainstorm within the rainstorm?" And then she stated, "I want you to paint about those times He communicated His Presence and love outside the typical situations. Paint those times and tell the stories, how He showed up in the midst of your grief."

I looked at Jody quizzically, "Really? I'm a novice painter, and I don't think I can pull it off!" She just stared at me, unflinching. I knew her well enough to know that she would keep insisting until I started in on her "assignment." I didn't really get her point, but—oh well—it seemed important to her that I at least consider what she was suggesting. I shrugged my shoulders and decided to give it a try.

Several weeks had passed since Jody had given me her painting assignment. I had mulled it over but kept putting it off, probably out of some ridiculous felt need to paint the perfect rainstorm, hummingbird, and red rose. I included Haystack Rock on the mental list as well.

At last I purchased a watercolor travel journal and a few more tubes of paint from Art Media, and after returning home with my new supplies I sat right down at my desk, in front of the window overlooking the golf course, to paint. Staring out the window, I considered my obligation to follow through with painting each image.

I thought about Haystack Rock, the one in Pacific City touted as Oregon's original (there is another rock by that name in Cannon Beach). I thought about the first anniversary of David's death and about how our family had been together at Pacific City for part of the day. I remembered how intentional we had been about being together, about how Jim and I had watched our grown "kids" running down the sand dunes, and about how we had laughed until our bellies ached on our drive home. I remembered how certain I had been of the Lord's Presence with us, both in the day's laughter and in its tears.

Then I recalled the spring day Elizabeth and I had cleaned up the deck and repotted some of the plants David and I had together purchased at Tony's Garden Center months earlier, when he had been home on leave from Iraq. My daughter and I had worked hard on that sunny day in April, and we'd also had some deep conversations about grieving David and about how I would have grieved just as deeply had the missing child been her or Jason or Daniel.

I recalled wiping away my tears as we repotted the plants David had picked out. It was hard to believe that had been less than a year earlier, and here we were once again shopping at Tony's Garden Center, this time for flowers and trees to bring some green to the deck.

Elizabeth and I finally sat down to take a break, my arms and feet aching with neuropathy pain from all the standing and working. We were gazing out over the trees when suddenly, only a few feet in front of us, a hummingbird had flown directly before our line of vision, hovering in place for several seconds before shooting so high into the air that we lost track of it. Then another hummingbird shot out of a nearby bush and repeated the mesmerizing dance. This pattern was repeated several times as Elizabeth and I, the appreciative audience, sat stunned. I hurried indoors to retrieve the book *Birds in Oregon* that Denise had given me a year earlier for my fiftieth birthday. Quickly turning to the page about hummingbirds, I read aloud that the "male hummingbird performs a spectacular pendulum-like flight over the perched female." It was a mating dance we had been witnessing, choreographed by the Creator. This was truly a gift from God, expressing his love for and joy over us even in the midst of our sorrow.

Now, some time later seated at my table poised to begin painting, I remembered also the day that would have been David's twenty-seventh birthday, the day on which I had gazed outside at 6:30 in the morning and spotted a full-blown red rose in early May. I believe that the Lord had again been expressing His love, assuring me of His knowledge of my broken heart on our son's birthday.

As I recalled all of those times, along with many others, when I had known the Lord was showing up to break through my fog of grief—to infiltrate and permeate my story with His Presence and His love—I began to worship. Song after song poured forth from my heart, and before I realized what I was doing I found myself facedown on the living room floor. I was facedown not because a crushing weight of grief had penetrated the ceiling and thrust me there but because I was on holy ground, and the Lord was meeting me there. Drawn to the book of Deuteronomy, I turned to chapter 33 and began reading verses 26–27: "There is no one like the God of Jeshurun, who rides across the heavens to help you and on the clouds in His majesty. The eternal God is your refuge, and underneath are the everlasting arms."

I read these compelling words over and over again, letting them wash over me with the knowledge of His Presence, with the almost palpable sensation of His arms underneath and around me, holding me. Those same arms had supported me in this same living room on September 13, 2004, when after hearing the news of David's death I had crumpled to the floor, screaming and seemingly unable to rise. His arms had been undergirding me all along since that moment, encircling me every time I cried out to Him, feeling as though my prayers were bouncing off the ceiling. And I had been locked in His embrace each time I had stood at David's grave.

His arms had upheld me those times when I had stood in church and tried in vain to sing, unable to form the words and with no melody flowing from my mouth. His grasp had enfolded me as I grappled and wrestled with pain, loss, and suffering and when the physical pain in my body kept me from doing anything other than sitting on the couch. His arms were underneath me, propping me up when I was laid off from my job in youth ministry. All along and in ever circumstance He had been my refuge, and even now He was and is holding me in His strong arms. His Presence is with me always.

I don't recall how long I lay prone on my living room floor, worshiping my Savior.

What I do know is that He met me there. He rode across the heavens and on the clouds to meet with me. And He opened the eyes of my heart in a new way, with the assurance that He is ever present with me in the midst of the trouble and pain and sorrow I carry. I leaned into Him and began as I worshipped to find and reclaim my voice. I leaned into Him and could hear once again the resounding notes of the music that had ceased for on the day I had lost my David. When I finally rose to my feet, I walked out onto the deck and gazed at the tall evergreens and the acres of green on the manicured golf course, acutely aware that the hue that had long since faded was clearer and crisper once again. The beauty of creation, so long muted, engulfed and transfixed me. I rejoiced and profusely thanked my Creator for the surfeit of beauty and joy all around me. I gladly received the healing balm that was washing over me.

The fog was dissipating, and as it lifted there was a settling in my heart and in my mind concerning those places in which the Lord had met me. I didn't dance off into the sunset and proclaim that I would now live happily ever after. Mine is not a happy-clappy, Disneyland faith that seeks to tie up everything in a neat little bow. My faith is sure, however, even in the midst of the heartache ensuing from my son's brutal demise. God's arms are underneath and His Presence is with me. I still cannot sing glib, syrupy songs, nor do I rashly make promise after promise to the Lord about how faithful I will be to Him. But I can and do worship with confidence, knowing experientially of His love and Presence even during the storms. Sometimes the words can't find their way out of my mouth, but my heart can sing with a sacrifice of worship as I meditate on words of praise and thankfulness to Jesus.

He alone has the power to dispel the seemingly impenetrable fog of grief that seeks to ground my spirit, preventing its flight. His is a tender power that lifts the punishing weight from my aching, benumbed shoulders and hefts it for me. It is a tender power that whispers assurances in my ear, even during the long, dark watches of the night when I soak the pillow with the tears of missing my son. It is a tender power, a Presence that stands with me at my son's graveside and holds me up, the borrowed strength of the Almighty One who gives me words of hope, not only for myself but to speak to others who also grieve. I sing a lament to Him, and He hears and holds me and promises never to let me go. The truth that lifts my lamenting heart from prone to vertical, from desperation to exaltation, is just this: He is with me. This is the truth that I have found and treasure.

His promise is a grace-song. As I read His Word, replete with pledges of His Presence and abiding love, the words are indeed like a grace-song sung over me. The melody breaks through my weariness and grief with the invitation to receive Him and all He has to offer, even in the midst of devastating sorrow.

He alone offers life and love, strength and truth, mercy and peace—a place to rest my weary head when I am worn out and parched from crying. The journey of grief and lament over David's death is not over yet, nor will it be this side of heaven. When my heart is breaking and my tears are flowing, however, Jesus invites me to taste the sweetness of His grace as He sings over me. In the unforgettable words of Zephaniah 3:17, "The LORD your God is with you, the Mighty Warrior who saves. He will take great delight in you;

in his love he will no longer rebuke you, but will rejoice over you with singing."

He was with us when our returning children met together in that intersection in Cannon Beach on the evening before Elizabeth's wedding. He was with us a month later, as well, when we heard the most horrific news of our lives.

His everlasting arms were and are beneath us, enveloping and upholding. And He places on our lips our own grace-song, perhaps intoned through tears of sorrow, even as He sees and weeps along with our tears of lament poured out over our soldier-son who from our earthly perspective left us too soon. I sense His Presence when I stand at David's grave, my eyes and heart gently tracing the *Gentle Warrior* etched there in the stone.

What a solace that the One who wept with Mary now weeps with me. His own grace-song is sung over me, expressed as He gives me the place and space to grieve and lament my son, without hurrying me along. He is with me now and through eternity. My comfort is in His holy, sacred Presence. It was He who broke through the fog of my grief with His tender power, intoning a grace-song over me. I am not alone.

God of Mystery, indeed!

# Chapter 16

# Labor Pains

I have witnessed the births of all three of Daniel and Adina's children, an honor and delight I treasure deeply. All three were different and unique. Aubie, the firstborn, was the first grandbaby on both sides of the family. Adina's doctor scheduled her to be induced on March 12. They were still living in Nebraska, so Jim and I booked tickets to fly there, along with Elizabeth and Erik.

Adina's labor was attended by family and a few close friends. She amazed me with her quiet and calm demeanor amid so much activity. I think I would have been completely undone by the sheer number of people in the labor room. Once it was time to push, all of the men except for Daniel were excused; they waited down the hall in a comfortable seating area, where they quickly gathered around a table and began playing cards.

All of the women, as well, were asked to leave momentarily while Adina was prepped for delivery. We waited together right outside her door—Elizabeth, Pam (Adina's mom), Briana (Adina's sister), her best friend Angie, and my cousin's wife Laurie.

I was deep in thought about this momentous occasion, marveling at the wonder of childbirth and the unique privilege of being present. Excitement was in the air, and I felt as though I could nearly burst. Then it hit me, the timing of it all, when we were all taking guesses about what time Aubie might arrive. I had already realized when the doctor set the date for Adina to be induced that this hadn't been by chance. It was exactly two and one half years from the date on which David had been killed—September 13, though it was still September 12 in the United States. And it was a Monday afternoon after 4:30.

Now here it was on a Monday afternoon, March 12, close to 4:00. As the realization overcame me I began to weep. Walking away quickly, I found a place where I could be alone. Elizabeth, not understanding what had set off the tears, walked over to see whether I was all right. The others didn't comprehend the significance of the time and date, but she did, and I was thankful for her presence. A peace settled over me as I felt once again that God's hand was on me and His powerful Presence with me. He knew the time of David's death. And now He opened my eyes to sense this new and tender touch on the lives of our family.

Soon the women were invited back into the delivery room, and we stood in the back, waiting, hoping, and praying. Elizabeth was at the head of Adina's bed, taking pictures at the couple's request. Pam and I, the grandmothers, were holding on to each other in shared excitement, looking at one another with unmasked anticipation, . . . and then Aubie was born—within ten minutes of the time, two and one half years earlier, that David had been killed. A redemption story was being woven into the fabric of our family; only God could have been behind such a "coincidence."

At that point the men, too, were invited back into the room. Jim, Adina's dad, and her great-grandpa hovered over Adina and Aubie. Adina held Aubie out to Jim, who beamed at the privilege of being the first to hold this first grandchild. Tears filled everyone's eyes as Jim offered her to the little one's great-grandpa, who in turn handed her to Adina's dad, . . . who walked over and offered her to me. I embraced the little one for a moment before handing her off to Pam, who in turn offered the tiny bundle to Elizabeth. From there the unsuspecting little one was passed along in turns to Briana, Angie, and Laurie, who bent down, with Aubie in her arms, so my wheel-chair-bound cousin Gary could gaze into the tiny face. The room was hushed as the holding and offering wove throughout the families. This joint welcoming of the newborn into the world marked one of the most holy, beautiful moments I've ever experienced. Her life is certainly an intimate gift from God.

When grandchild number two came along, Daniel and Adina were informed that they would be having another girl in mid-September. Because some other questions were raised at the time, another ultrasound was scheduled for a few weeks later, and Adina invited me along to the appointment. They were now living in Portland, in our home, after having moved from Nebraska nearly a year earlier.

We were unprepared for the news we heard during this ultrasound. Despite assuming the earlier gender verdict to be correct, Daniel shared with us later that he had been praying for the determination to have been mistaken; he was sure they would be having a boy. As we watched the picture on the screen of their unborn child, the technician quipped, "It looks like you'll want to do some shopping; you probably won't want your baby boy in your daughter's clothes!" We were elated, and tears of joy began streaming down Daniel's face. Little Aubie was becoming a little loud and restless, so Daniel took her from the room. It should have been me taking her out, I realized belatedly. In another moment, though, I was once again to be taken aback by an intimate touch of the Father's hand.

The tech started talking to Adina and me about a new due date, announcing casually, "It looks like your little guy is due on . . . yep . . . It looks like his due date is . . . September 13." Adina locked eyes with me, her own growing wide as saucers. I looked back at her, incredulous. How could this be? *Please Lord, not on this day of death,* was my first thought. I kept shaking my head and murmuring to myself, *What just happened? How can this be true?*

We had taken separate cars to the appointment, so afterward I walked out, dreamlike, to my own. It all felt so unreal, to hear this particular date related to the birth of our grand . . . *son?!* Two huge surprises in one day. I could hardly hold myself together. As soon as I had made my way to my car I called Jim.

My husband, too, was incredulous when he heard the newly updated news, exclaiming, "This is crazy!! They're having a *boy* now?! *AND HE'S DUE SEPTEMBER 13?!*" He conceded to me later that he had felt confused and alarmed upon realizing that our grandson's due date coincided with that of our David's demise. After we said our goodbye he called our pastor, Rick, explaining what had taken place. Jim was ecstatic about the prospect of welcoming a grandson, not to mention the knowledge that Daniel and Adina had already announced their intention to name him Lincoln David in honor of his departed uncle. The part Jim felt was messing with his head, as it was my own, was the projected due date of September 13. "Rick," Jim protested, "This is crazy shit! What in the world?! Is God playing a game with us?" To which Rick, with his calm and wise demeanor, responded with alacrity, "Jim, This is crazy beautiful! This is another redemption story!"

After Jim's conversation with Rick, he immediately called me back to announce that he wanted to meet me for lunch. At the restaurant he shared with me Rick's response, to which I readily agreed. This was indeed one crazy beautiful redemption story!

A few months later, on August 31, Lincoln David entered the world. He had decided to arrive early, just as his Uncle David had done thirty years earlier. Daniel sobbed unabashedly when his son was born, knowing as he did that this little one was to be named after his own brother who couldn't have been present to share in his joy. Another holy moment was recorded in my memory book as I witnessed Daniel and Adina welcoming their newborn son into their family. Again Elizabeth was there, helpful as usual, snapping pictures and sharing in their joy. Adina's friend Megan and her sister-in-law, Cindy, joined us in the delivery room. We had Adina's mom on the phone during the delivery.

Sometime after Lincoln David turned one year old our daughter, Elizabeth, and her husband, Erik, were expecting their own firstborn. A few months into her pregnancy we learned that she was carrying twin boys—just as I once had! What fun for a mother and a daughter to share in the experience of carrying and delivering twin sons. Elizabeth needed to be on bed rest in the last few months of her pregnancy, and this was at times stressful to her. She understandably wanted to have those babies born as close to her early June due date as possible, but the closer it got to the end of May the more I struggled with ambivalent feelings. What if the boys were born on Memorial weekend? Would this seemingly unfortunate timing overshadow their birthday celebrations year after year? I wanted so deeply, for all our sakes, for her sons' date of birth to be unfettered by any association with the sadness Memorial weekend can bring. Both her wedding and her birthday were already indelibly marked with their closeness to the anniversary of David's death.

Memorial weekend came, . . . and with it her precious boys, Elliott and Silas. Elizabeth was one courageous woman, following in her mom's footsteps with a natural childbirth without meds. The pain was excruciating, though the gift of her long-awaited sons clearly outshone her extreme discomfort. What pure joy to hold, along with Erik's parents, those precious, tiny bundles. Our elation was full, and we were mutually grateful for the safe and healthy delivery of these little guys. We were incredibly grateful for the gift of life times two, especially on Memorial weekend.

Three years later Adina was in labor with her third child. As with all the other births of my grandchildren, I felt as though I were being given a sacred gift in the ability to meet yet another newly minted infant even as her first breath filled the air sacs of her waiting lungs.

As I sat with Adina during her labor with Quinnleigh, I remembered one of the first things my grief counselor, Cindy, had shared with me during a counseling session: "Grief is like the ebb and flow of contractions during labor. The pain comes and goes. We can't control it. If we're experiencing a contraction, the only thing we need to do is breathe with it, allow it to be there, acknowledge it, and try not to fight the pain. If we're in a 'resting phase' of grief or labor it's all right to move, to resume normal activities, and to talk or laugh or just be ourselves. In other words, be wherever you are in your grief, and try to be as present as possible in what you're experiencing. Your grief can be trusted to take you where you need to go."

Labor pains are certainly unpleasant, uncomfortable, and exhausting. Yet riding along with and going through the pain is the only option. It's impossible to get around it.

Labor is the track to delivering a child into this world.

Grief is painful.

Grief is uncomfortable.

Grief is exhausting.

To grieve in a healthy way one must face it head on.

We do have some short-term options, but ignoring grief or glossing over it doesn't bring healing.

Grief is the only track that points in the direction of healing.

After that initial appointment with my counselor I thought about those first few days and weeks following David's death. Grief had weighed heavily on me, to be sure, like a shroud of thick, dark thick fog threatening to envelop me. The pain in my heart had been so piercing I had felt as though I could hardly breathe. I had felt hopeless, looking in dismay at the growing stack of books on our bookshelf on the subject of grief, some of which I had received from well-meaning friends. Most of the time in those early days I couldn't bring myself to read more than a chapter before feeling overwhelmed. Cindy had assured me, "This is normal, too."

At times I would try to concentrate on only a few paragraphs and end up in tears. Certain books I literally threw across the floor; others I rejected based on their simplistic answers. None of them came close to touching, let alone healing, the agony I was enduring. I couldn't imagine finding my way, with or without their help, to the other side of the despair I felt. While I conceded that some were helpful—even very helpful—my concentration level was anything but sharp. This loss of focus, too, Cindy reassured me, was to be expected. I wondered, frustrated, why I couldn't seem to read more than a few pages without getting bored, distracted, or upset. I wondered whether I would ever again be able to engage with reading, one of my favorite pastimes.

I only wanted to sleep.

My body ached, my job had been terminated, and David wouldn't be coming home in March of o-five with the rest of the Oregon National Guard's 2nd Battalion, 162nd Infantry.

During those first few months nothing had felt "normal." I was living in a new home and in a new neighborhood, driving to new grocery stores and taking a new route to church. My full work schedule had been replaced by putting in only occasional hours. It felt grueling, anyway, to go back to my office at church ever aware that my job would be ending soon. On other days, when I went into the office I couldn't help but notice that the burden wasn't as heavy; planning an event for the girls seemed fun for a few days. The ebb and flow of grief . . .

A few weeks after David died our family members went back to their normal commitments—Jason to Camp Pendleton, Daniel to school in Nebraska, and Elizabeth to work here in Portland. Jim eventually went back to work, as well. Mostly home, I numbly slogged through the days.

We would receive occasional calls from Herb saying that another box with David's personal belongings had arrived from Iraq. "When would be a good time for me to bring it over?" We always waited until Jim was home from work. Caleb Mayhew, we knew, had helped pack the boxes at Camp Taji, and we found comfort in knowing that our son's personal items had been touched lovingly and kindly by a friend. On some of his clothes I detected his particular scent, and I held them close, breathing in what still smelled like David.

After the initial shock of receiving the news, Cathy and Clark had spent the first few nights with us. Upon entering our guest room they had encountered some of David's clothing, still lying on the bed from when he had been on leave. Solemnly they brought us the clothing he had so recently left behind: a shirt and a pair of pants, the outfit out of which he had changed when putting on his Army fatigues for traveling back to Iraq. Right away on the discarded clothing I noticed the scent of his musky aftershave and cologne.

Oftentimes during those first few days and weeks I would lie on the swing outside and hug those still unwashed clothes tightly to my chest, breathing in what was left of his scent. The swing was situated on the south end of the deck, overlooking the hilly, lush green golf course. But it wouldn't have made a difference if the view had been a brick wall. My senses had been progressively dulled by sorrow and a lack of sleep. Color, beauty, music . . . the intrigue of it all had faded away. The ebb and flow of grief, I knew, needed to wash over me, and I had to face the pain.

Our black lab, Pete, was often by my side. Once, while we were out on the swing with me clutching David's blue shirt, Pete enterprisingly brought me one of his toys, a big rubber tire, which he strategically positioned next to my face. I had to chuckle at the mental machinations of this sweet dog who knew I was sad and thought his toy might help. Another time I was lying on the swing with a blanket covering me. It was fall and starting to get chilly outside. Pete gently lifted the top of the blanket with his teeth and took it off me, prodding me to get up. I complied, much to his doggie delight.

On some of those days when the pain and heaviness of grief nearly consumed me, I wrestled with questions about my personal value. I had absolutely no energy to look for another position in my chosen area of youth ministry. The idea of looking for another job, in that field or any other, seemed close to impossible. My body ached all of the time, and my accommodative husband was handling almost everything that needed to be done around the house. I couldn't concentrate on anything for very long. And I felt angry—enraged, even. Robbed of David, robbed by death. And robbed of meaningful work, as well. What did I have to offer my family and friends—or anyone else? I was fifty years old, and I felt as though my life was over.

Lament poured out of my weary soul: "How long, Lord, how long? Will my heart always ache this much? Will the pain ever subside? Will this dark night pass? What is on the other side?"

I clung to the hope of seeing David again someday. This had been instilled in my heart from an early age, and I believed it to be true and found it reassuring, but the sadness, grief, and loss still overwhelmed me. Rummaging through some old drawings from the kids when they were little, I found one of David's renditions, declaring in awkward block letters that he loved Jesus, his Savior. The expression of his childlike faith precipitated grateful tears.

I was facing my pain and missing my son. I had accepted, at least intellectually, that I would live out the rest of my earthly life without him. So would Jim. Our grandchildren would never know their Uncle David. Elizabeth, Jason, and Daniel missed their brother terribly.

Again, the scene in my living room played itself out: a warm and beautiful summer day punctuated by the incongruous sight of two soldiers walking into our home and telling us the worst possible news about our David. I would scream in my head,

"GET OUT!!"

"GO BACK!!"

"DON'T SPEAK!!"

Would that loop ever stop repeating? Would the outcome ever change?

Just as my counselor, Cindy, had prepared me, I couldn't control the trajectory of my grief. I simply had to breathe in synch with its peaks and valleys, to force myself not to fight the pain. As I practiced being present with my grief, I started reading from the book of Lamentations. When I reached the third chapter I marveled that Jeremiah, the writer, had been so spot on. I echoed his lament. "[B]ecause of His great love, we are not consumed" washed over me with waves of comfort and reassurance.

> *"I have been deprived of peace; I have forgotten what prosperity is.*
>
> *I remember my affliction and my wandering, the bitterness and the gall.*
>
> *I well remember them and my soul is cast down within me.*
>
> *Yet this I call to mind and therefore, I have hope:*
>
> *Because of the LORD's great love we are not consumed, for His compassions never fail. They are new every morning, great is your faithfulness.*
>
> *I say to myself, The LORD is my portion; therefore I will wait for Him."*
>
> *Lamentations 3:17–24*

It was as though Jeremiah had been reading my mind. I wouldn't fall into the black hole of despair. I had hope. I wouldn't be completely consumed, and the Lord did have never-ending compassion for me. To know His love for me was and is a gift eternal, and to know in those early months that I wouldn't be completely undone was a grace-song being sung over me. The shroud of grief seemed lighter after I had engaged with Lamentations 3. Was this what Cindy meant when she had talked about the ebb and flow of grief? Sometimes the pain of mourning would seem relentless, and then the load would seem unaccountably to lighten.

A few months after David's death Erik's parents invited us to stay in their home at the beach over a weekend while they were out of town. We decided to take them up on their offer and brought two other dear couples along with us. Our friends were gracious, and as we cycled through the rise and fall of the pain they made room in their hearts for the undulations. As we gazed through the windows there in Arch Cape, overlooking the Pacific, we idly watched the choreographed movement, the rhythmic advance and retreat, of the ocean waves below us. Just as we were powerless to pause the thrust of the waves on the beach, so we were unable to harness our pain.

We tentatively spoke to our friends about our grief, and they shared, as well, what was on their hearts. It was all so fresh and welcome—new territory to navigate with our friends. This weekend wasn't all about us, for there was an underlying rhythm of reciprocation, of giving and receiving, an intricate weaving of stories and of grief and of "resting phases." Our circle in that beach home included our children, though none of them was at the time physically present; they had grown up together, and these friends had been with us at the Railtons' home a few short months earlier to commemorate Elizabeth's wedding. It made sense the way we were all overcome at times, seated together now in this place with our memories of the wedding and of family and pictures and goodbyes. The declaration of Lamentations 3 echoed again: "because of the LORD's great love, we are not consumed."

Thank you, Jeremiah; you spoke your heart with an authenticity that rings true and deeply touches my broken heart in a way that uniquely lends itself to the birth of healing and hope and to a deeper experience of the Father's love.

*Chapter 17*

# Nail Salon

A broken story, intertwined with a grace-song, was spoken in an unlikely place, though it initially seemed self-focused. On this particular day I walked into the nail salon alone, only to walk out somewhat later with a heavy heart and a lament forming on my lips.

Typically, my friend and I met to have our nails done. This was an escape from the harshness of reality, a deliberate decision to do something kind for myself, as well as to see my friend and hear about her life. We were also getting to know our manicurists as new friends. I always set my appointment with a particular young man in his thirties; he was funny, polite, kind, and respectful, and I suspect he enjoyed chatting with a "mother figure." On the day I went in without my friend I heard his story and came to understand why he might have been moved to confide in a woman who had suffered.

He started out by asking the whereabouts of my friend, to which I responded that she was sick and so unable to meet for our regular appointment. He took my hand, looked me in the eye, and announced meaningfully, "Then I will tell you my story today, Marilyn."

As I listened intently to this brave young man, the snippets of his story coordinating with the filings, trimming, and polishing, hot tears rolled down my face.

He had grown up in Vietnam, and when he was twelve his parents had sacrificed all of their savings, along with their hearts, to place him on a boat to flee the country with strangers who promised to bring him to the USA. He was their only child, their beloved son, and they desired more than anything else for him to grow up in freedom.

Jounced about with the waves in an overcrowded boat in the South China Sea for weeks before landing in Malaysia, he was taken upon arrival to a refugee camp. On the boat he had grown up fast, witnessing horrific crimes against the hapless female passengers—not to mention even murders, robberies, and drownings.

At the camp his loneliness grew, and he yearned for home and the embrace of his parents, remembering their sacrifice and soldiering on to make them proud. One day, six months after arriving at the camp, he at last received a letter from home. Running down to the nearby river for a few moments of privacy, he squatted on the shore and read the letter over and over again, tears streaming down his face. They spoke of their love for their only child and of their desire for him to have better opportunities in a free country. Frightened of being discovered in a weakened state and suffering ridicule or, worse, being taken advantage of, he continuously looked over his shoulder to make sure no one was coming his way.

Eventually, my young friend made it to the USA in the company of a new best friend. The two learned English together and finished their education, and after meeting his future wife, he traveled with her from Los Angeles to Portland to start the business in which he is currently engaged. They now have three of the cutest little girls I've ever seen. To this day he hasn't been reunited his parents. It had been more than twenty years since he last saw them, though he regularly writes letters and speaks with them on the phone.

He expressed how grateful he was for his parents and for their sacrifice—profoundly thankful as well for the privilege of living in a free country and enjoying, without fear, his life with his wife and daughters.

At this point in the narrative he stopped working, grasped my hand, and looked me straight in the eye. He had seen my tears over what he had endured as a child, and now he turned around and blessed me. Looking at me with a tenderness almost belied by his strong voice, he asserted, "Marilyn, you be proud of your son! Your son sacrificed his life for me and people like me. You be proud of your son!"

A sob of tsunami proportions was welling up within me. Following my appointment I drove straight up the hill to Willamette National Cemetery, only a mile away. At David's grave I dropped to my knees, weeping not for myself or for my own deceased son but for my Vietnamese friend and his parents, bereft not, thankfully, through the separation of death but through an interminable gap of miles. I wept with gratitude for a friendship forged and a broken story shared. I wept with gratefulness for having been entrusted with such a story, and I prayed for hope and healing in this young man's life. I wept with a deepening gratefulness for a noble soldier son who had dared to give his life so that others might find the freedoms he had throughout that life so thoroughly enjoyed.

And a lament poured out from me for all the stories still unspoken.

My friend's saga and his words of thankfulness spoken to me constituted an unexpected grace-song, a gift I would treasure. God showed up that day at the nail salon, and I am marked with a deeper and more lasting beauty than could ever have been effected through a simple manicure. I am marked by the beauty of seeing and having been seen.

# Chapter 18

# The Long and Loopy Hot Pink Waterslide

**B**ucket list
Syllabification: (buck·et list) *noun informal* "a number of experiences or achievements that a person hopes to have or accomplish during their lifetime: *"making this trip is the first thing on my bucket list."*

The idea of creating a bucket list was daunting, and I gave up on it before I even seriously tried. I resisted the idea, fearing that my health would prevent me from any attempts to accomplish what I might set out to do. I resisted until I saw

the

long

and

loopy

hot

pink

waterslide.

*Could I? Would I?*

The chronic nerve pain in my feet and legs kept me from enjoying a simple walk, from standing and talking with friends at a party or at church, and from browsing at Saturday Market in downtown Portland. My sister found a lightweight wheelchair for me to use when I went anywhere outside my home, though I resisted taking it to church and instead sat most of the time when I was there. If I attended a performance or play and didn't bring the wheelchair, I sat near the doorway and felt panicky if I had to stand and wait for too long to either enter or exit. It was like that everywhere I went. I estimated how far I might have to walk and how long I'd have to stand, and then, based on my calculations, would decide whether or not I could realistically attend the play, performance, football game, or graduation ceremony. I missed my nephew's high school graduation prior to obtaining the wheelchair because it would have been too far for me to walk into the building.

I couldn't manage to walk up my driveway and across the street uphill to visit my friend Renee. Though she lived only a short distance away, I would have had to negotiate on foot the two-hundred-foot elevation between my home and hers; fortunately, I was able to drive to her home.

The weight of navigating a lifestyle with such tight parameters kept me at home more often than not. Already in deep grief, I found the factor of physical disability an overwhelming obstacle. I felt stuck and was losing hope for any remedy to restore a measure of my health. What I heard from my neurologist and read about my degenerative nerve disorder was this: "It will worsen, and your life will be limited." I noted that it was important to try to exercise and keep a positive mindset, but I lacked the energy for either.

I took all sorts of medicines prescribed by the neurologist, but after several years when nothing else was working he put me on a very low dose of a timed-release morphine for the pain. The pros: it enabled me to walk with little pain, and even to eventually go back to the gym. I could also go grocery shopping and prepare meals, stand and talk to friends at a party or at church, and hold my newborn grandchildren. The cons of taking morphine every day for years: I was sleepy most of the time (depending on the time of day, I could close my eyes and be asleep within a minute, especially when reading). I had to be extremely careful about driving, and, after I had taken morphine daily for six years, my digestion issues became a constant battle.

I did some research about other means for managing chronic nerve pain and learned about different vitamins, herbs, and supplements I could take to o alleviate the pain. I also did some circuit training. As I worked through my grief, both with Cindy and on my own, those gains too led to a healthier outlook. My emotional and physical pain were intrinsically intertwined.

A friend asked me to trust her before taking me to visit a physical therapist whose methodology was fairly unknown, though touted as successful. He was the first medical professional who gave me hope for my future. His father suffered from the same disorder with which I had been diagnosed and was finding relief. I began to see this therapist twice a month for nearly two years, during which I kept improving. He also talked to me about eliminating certain items from my diet, which made a difference, as well.

At the same time my grief counselor, Cindy, was helping me with the memories that so traumatized me—particularly those of the two soldiers in dress uniform walking purposefully into our home and telling us the news of David's death. That traumatic memory thrust itself insistently into my consciousness over and over again, unbidden and unwelcome and pulling me down into the place of deepest grief. Cindy helped me with a reprocessing therapy known as EMDR, Eye Movement Desensitization and Reprocessing, which is commonly used in therapy with people suffering from Post-Traumatic Stress Syndrome.

In the words of the licensed mental health counselor Cindy Brosh, "In EMDR therapy, specific patterns of the eye movement, auditory cues or tactile sensations (or a combination of these), are guided by the therapist. These unlock the nervous system and allow the brain to process the experience using both left and right hemispheres. The client is in control of the process, while the therapist acts as a guide. Locked-in, disturbing memories can be stored in isolated memory networks of the brain. This prevents learning from taking place regarding the original event. In another part of the brain, in a separate network, is most of the information that is needed to resolve the isolated memory material. So, the old material just keeps getting triggered over and over again. Once EMDR processing begins, the two networks are allowed to link together. New information can then come into consciousness and resolve the trauma and negative beliefs associated with it."

The EMDR therapy helped to disarm my memories of the two soldiers walking into my home with their cruel message. Ultimately the scene was replaced, whenever I was triggered, with a new and comforting vision: a gorgeous setting in Maui I find peaceful. I am immensely grateful to Cindy and her wise, devoted work with me.

By the grace of God, and with a combination of doing my grief work, EMDR, exercise, vitamins, herbs, supplements, diet, physical therapy, and prayer, my life was changing and my body beginning to mend. The triggers that had recurrently led me back to the living room scene no longer held power over me. I has also allied myself with a new physician who became the second medical professional to hold out the hope that I could stop taking morphine and keep managing my health without such a strong medicine. With her help I successfully made the transition off of morphine eight years after David's death, and I am now feeling well . . . which leads me to the long and loopy hot pink waterslide!

As a little girl I became fearful of water. My mother and my older sister had both been deathly afraid of water from the time they were young, and my mother used to inform me in a tone of finality, "The Holforty girls are all afraid of the water." My mother's maiden name was Holforty; she had grown up on a farm in rural South Dakota with one brother and four sisters, and she and her sisters had referred to themselves as the "Holforty girls." She had shared with me that they were all shy and afraid to swim: my older sister had grown up with this phobia, as had several of my cousins. You can see the self-perpetuating pattern; I, too, by suggestion and default, was terrified of water. Still, as a child I had determined to face my fear and learn to swim. Since my parents resisted spending money on anything they deemed unnecessary, swimming lessons were out of the question.

When I was in the seventh grade I nearly died three times. Once I was stung by a bee—it was through the aftermath of that experience that I learned I was allergic. I anxiously walked home from the park, one block from my home, after having trouble breathing. My parents, unaware of the urgency, did take me to the doctor . . . at a somewhat convenient time for them. This was near the end of the day, and they brought me in through the back door of the clinic they were hired to clean after hours. Clearly unaware of the gravity of an allergic reaction to a bee sting, they were gratified by the doctor's willingness to see me on a gratis basis. Soon after treatment I was breathing normally again.

The other two instances in which I nearly died both involved water. I was out on the Colombia River with my older sister and her family, playing in shallow water with her children, when I drifted into deeper water and began flailing about, literally fighting for my life. My nieces and nephew, thinking that I was playing, broke into laughter, and I to this day don't know why my sister and brother-in-law failed to notice. My nephew, who was only about eight years old at the time, eventually pulled me to safety.

The second time I nearly drowned was at a swim club to which my friends belonged. A group of us were sitting on the edge of the pool around the six-foot mark when a boy pushed me into the water. I seriously saw my life flash before my eyes. A friend who knew I couldn't swim pulled me to safety, but I was terrified. After arriving back home, I told my parents I had once again nearly drowned and insisted that I needed to learn to swim.

Later on they did sign me up for lessons at the local YMCA. I attended the first three sessions but was terrified of putting my face into the water—too frightened, in fact, to try almost anything I was instructed to do. My fear was so intense that I skipped out of class nearly every week. My parents didn't have a clue; my dad would take me to the lessons, drop me off, and return later on to pick me up. In the meantime I would hide out in the locker room, making sure to get my hair wet so I would appear to have been in the water. They never did catch on or ask to see me swim. This "Holforty girl" had learned to deceive.

Years later the Lord began a healing work in me. I became less fearful of the water after several trips to Maui. Seven years after David died Jim and I renewed our vows in Kauai, at Ha'ena State Park, where lush tropical jungles meet white sand beaches and turquoise water. And I snorkeled in

Kauai for the first time in my life, using a flotation device to keep me buoyant. Jim and I held hands in the waters off Poipu Beach, and I witnessed firsthand the incredible beauty and peacefulness of which my husband had spoken for years.

On a cold January afternoon back in Portland, Jim and I were at the nearby indoor water park watching our grandchildren and their parents splash and play in the water. It hadn't occurred to me to bring our suits and join in the fun, so we sat on the sidelines. This usually this wasn't a bummer, but today was different. My family members were playing in shallow water, of course, and we could easily have joined in the fun. We strolled over to where they were splashing, and I noticed that the area into which the waterslides dumped their riders was only four feet deep. Looking up at the twin waterslides, I noted that one was enclosed; the other, the long and loopy hot pink slide, on the other hand, was open. I glanced at Jim and announced without preamble, "I need to add this waterslide to my bucket list!" My husband was, understandably, quite surprised. After all, we had dated in high school and married in our early twenties, and all along he had been well aware of my inordinate fear of water. He also knew, of course, that some deep healing had taken place in my life—physically, emotionally, and spiritually. I remarked glibly, "Why not today? Is there any reason I shouldn't go down the waterslide? Will you go with me?" He immediately responded in the affirmative, before racing home to grab our suits and towels.

After Jim's return we quickly changed into our suits and headed up to the top of the waterslide. Our grandchildren waited expectantly on the other side of the rope that divides the play area from that at the bottom of the slide.

As we climbed the stairs my legs felt like rubber, and I almost wanted to back out. But even as my heart beat faster I continued moving resolutely forward. We being the only grandparents in line, I started to feel a little foolish. However, with Jim's encouragement I held my ground. He would go first and wait at the bottom for me.

When my turn came I was shaking and my teeth were chattering. I stepped woodenly onto the long and loopy, hot pink waterslide. Jim had coached me in advance to stay upright to prevent my going as fast. *That* advice most certainly didn't work! The velocity pushed me backward, and off I went. Down the slide, to the left and quickly to the right and back to the left again. I was tossed all over the slide, terrified that I might somehow manage to fly up and out of its narrow perimeters. I went through loop after loop, feeling absolutely disoriented as I plunged into the water at the bottom. Once submerged and unable to orient myself in space, I began to fret, flail, and choke, taking in water in my panic. Where was Jim? What was happening? It didn't occur to me that I was in only four feet of water. What did occur to me was that I was terrified.

Looking up once my head had resurfaced, I spotted Jim nearby, calmly reaching out to me and touching my hand. As soon as our hands touched I stopped flailing and stood up . . . in four feet of water. I looked around, embarrassed, taking in my grandchildren with their eyes wide and mouths agape.

"Meme, are you okay?" the little ones asked in real concern. I laughed a little before responding in the affirmative. I didn't want to scare them, even belatedly. As I walked over to the side of the pool, I wanted to somehow disappear, even as my embarrassment grew. It was then that I looked up at the long and loopy hot pink waterslide . . . and started to giggle. I had done it! The outcome wasn't ideal, and it certainly wasn't pretty, but I'd done it! Scratch waterslide off the bucket list! Maybe I was losing my status as a fearful "Holforty girl" after all.

Later that evening I reminisced about the big event of the day, about my flailing and fretting in four feet of water, and about how Jim had calmly touched my hand and I had stood up. It seemed significant in retrospect that he hadn't taken my hand and pulled me up.

My thoughts took me back to another wintry day when I had contemplated painting some of the ways in which God had broken in to my story with His love. They reverted back to the outcome of my lying prostrate on the living room floor, worshiping God and coming to the realization that He was always with me.

Indeed, His Arms were underneath me, holding me through every storm, every dark night, and every deep valley—I guessed that applied to deep (and not quite so deep) pools as well. He hadn't promised to take away my pain, or my terror, but He was with me in and through it. There is great power in the Presence of God—unexplainable healing power and an impermeable peace in the midst of trouble.

My free-flowing thoughts took me back further then, to another day, to another scene in the same living room. To that day about which I used to return mentally over and over again, with torturing thoughts that threatened to take control of my mental processes. To the day those two Army officers in dress uniform arrived to conveys the news of David's death. I relived two stunning experiences in the same room, both of them turning points in my life. Reversing the pictures to their appropriate chronological order, I considered the first—that of the two uninvited guests with their devastating, unwanted news, as well as of the ensuing weight of grief that had come crashing through the ceiling, threatening to crush and suffocate me. The second was that picture of lying facedown in worship of the God who had ridden across the heavens, on the clouds in His majesty, to lift me in strong and gentle arms and transport me into the stratosphere, far above the bleak depths of my grief and lament. No, He hadn't come with all the answers, nor had he brought my David back to me. What He had brought was Himself and all the love, compassion, grace, and mystery He embodies. He touched me. He rescued me from the dark places and brought me into the light. When I was flailing before Him, He waited patiently for me to receive His healing, to reach out for His finger and receive from that healing touch the  strength to stand firm.

There can be no doubt that we live in a broken, messed up world. Brokenness surrounds us in our relationships and systems. We are inundated with horrific stories of human trafficking, mental illness, terrorist attacks, and refugee crises. It makes no sense when a five-year-old or young mother succumbs to cancer or a young man perishes in war. I don't pretend to understand how, or why, God allows these achingly horrific circumstances—though I know full well He neither initiates nor condones them. I can't begin to understand, either, why He also gives us grace as we wrestle with the questions of faith in times of great hardship and pain. How am I to live in relationship with such a wild, mysterious God?

It seems absurd to me to try to reason, to attempt to figure Him out or to posit answers. I used to think, especially in my younger years when I was enrolled in Bible college, that we Christians did in fact have all the answers. I was filled with arrogance. It occurs to me now that human pride leaves little room for faith in the God of Mystery, the God who pledges His Presence and His peace but makes no promise to give us all the answers. Not even when a son is brutally killed in a war against terrorism.

As I have wrestled through these issues of faith, grappling with that perennial human question of where God is in the midst of suffering and tragedy, I have stepped into the life of lament. I have joined in with the prayers of biblical lamenters, have seen that lament is woven throughout the Bible and that its language is breathtakingly beautifully. Some of the laments in the psalms are painfully scribed, etched in sorrow and tears—and all the more beautiful for it.

In my grief and sorrow over David, my health, and the loss of my career in youth ministry, I found the language of lament and leaned into it to find my voice. The Lord gave me a wide open space in which to grieve and wove into that space the beauty of His patience, Presence, understanding, and comfort.

# Chapter 19

# Finding My Voice

Outside my kitchen window I watch the hummingbirds taste sweet nectar as I prepare a meal or wash up some dishes. The tiny birds flit swiftly back and forth from their safe haven in a nearby tree.

When I first hung the hummingbird feeder I believed the sightings of these sweet birds would be seasonal. Then, as I stood at the window on Christmas Eve, I watched with amazement as one bird drank deeply from the nectar. Rather than flying quickly away, he flew to a branch directly in front of me and rested. I stood transfixed, reminding myself to breathe as I observed the compact creature perched before me. He sat there briefly and then started preening, meticulously cleaning each of his many feathers. I watched with fascination and awe as this tiny bird perched and preened a few feet from my kitchen window.

The presence of the hummingbird spoke to me of love and of the Presence of the Holy One. The One who loves me and knows my name. The presence of the hummingbird was like a reminder of the One who fashioned this lovely creature—the One called Creator.

Each time I gaze through the window and see a hummingbird at the feeder, I stop and watch with gratitude. This isn't a seasonal offering but a continuous reminder of God's Presence and love. I am reminded of the deeper story this creature brings to me, of that grace-song sung by the Creator over me. He sings His love, His presence, His beauty, and His redemption. He sings songs of restoration over a life broken, and He sings with the words of hope and healing.

There is a most beautiful verse in the Old Testament, in Malachi 4:2: "But for you who revere My name, the sun of righteousness will rise with healing in its wings. And you will go out and leap like calves released from the stall."

Yes, there is healing in these wings whirring before me, as the tiny creature points me to his Creator, the God who loves us both. The hummingbird's presence points me to the God who has shown up and broken through my story with His abiding love—that ultimate, impossible grace-song. Though the hummingbird flits to and fro and doesn't tarry long while feeding, I am filled with the awareness that the love and Presence of my Healer-God are a constant. He is with me, and it is this profound truth that suffuses my troubled soul with His inexplicable peace. As I trek the journey of grief and lament, His Presence and love are both the source and the depository of my hope.

In the early weeks and months after David's death I couldn't imagine finding a place of peace or rest, even though I knew Jesus as my Savior. Now, after walking through the dark night of my soul and knowing experientially that my faithful God will never leave or forsake me, I rest in Him. No, He hasn't altered my circumstances or taken away the pain of my son's early death, but He is with me as I endure its aftermath. That truth changes everything, and it has changed me in a profound and irreversible way.

The truth that lifts my lamenting heart from prostration to exaltation is this: He is with me. The question is *Will I come to Him and rest in Him? He kindly offers, but will I trust Him?*

My friend articulated this eloquently in a December sermon she preached at Imago Dei:

"In Christ we have the revelation of God's incarnation. He is with us. When all have left and we feel so terribly alone, He breaks through our story with this truth: He is with us."

This is life-changing truth. Truth that offers life-changing hope. In the midst of our horrific storms, He brings hope. Without the hope I have in Jesus I would stay in bed . . . or worse. I couldn't possibly go on living without Him. It is Jesus who enlightens the eyes of my heart to the grace and truth of Deuteronomy 33:27: "He is my refuge, and underneath are the everlasting arms."

What does this hope look like—for me, specifically, as a mom who has buried a soldier son? One might ask how I can possibly place my faith in the God of Mystery, the One who seems aloof and unaware of the tragedies about which we read daily, like when a son is brutally killed in war.

The reality is that I do cry out, with a heart broken, "Why haven't You intervened, God? You could have; You have the power to intervene. You have the power to still the raging seas and thwart the attempts of men intent on perpetrating evil." I don't have the answers, nor do neat or easy answers exist. I do know that He doesn't plan or desire for these tragedies to occur. I also know that He can turn something so horrific, so terribly tragic, into a story of redemption.

Will my eyes be attuned to God's redemption stories in the midst of the destruction? Will I wait on Him? There have been times I've become weary in the waiting.

If God is indeed with us, and His outstretched arms undergird us, how does this truly help? How does the heart filled with unspeakable pain transform into a heart able to find rest in the midst of that agony? What does it mean to place our faith and trust in a God who doesn't necessarily provide us the answers we want, with the outcomes or solutions for which we plead? Will we trust even so in the God of Mystery? Will we once again call Him good and worship with eyes wide open to this truth, even when pain, sorrow, and tragedy touch our lives? Will we sing to His Name the sacred songs of lament? Does He lament with us over these tragedies? To each nuance of these existential questions I answer with a resounding, unequivocal *yes!* I have known and continue to know the incarnate Christ to be the One who weeps and laments with us, as He did with Mary of Bethany. No, He doesn't barge into our lament with a "fix it" mentality. Nor does He glibly brush us off with a dismissive, "Stop crying—you'll see him again someday."

He doesn't shame us as we lament our personal losses or join the lament over the losses of others in this world.

Precisely how does Jesus, the Light of the world, enlighten you and me? How does He bring us hope? How does His Light break through the darkness of our grief and bring redemption when all around and within us seems so terribly dark and broken?

Speaking for myself, I can attest that He has sung His grace-song over me and has opened my eyes to redemption in the midst of my deepest angst. When a grace-filled story is woven into tragedy, through the brokenness a brighter glory shines, the glory of a heart filled with the brilliance of Christ›s enduring love. He has given me the strength to speak of the wounds of my heart, to bring them out and lay them bare. Only love and grace have the power to touch and begin to heal a wounded heart. No fluffy, *fa-la-la* faith can carry us through those moments when we seriously think we would rather die than live another minute with the relentless sorrow pushing down on us a weight nearly intolerable to bear in our own strength.

The wonder is that even as He redeems tragedies He also empowers us to speak truth and hope by His grace. I've heard, for example, of how He has empowered others to come alongside the women and children of the Congo to provide care, provision, and training to lift them out of dire poverty and hopelessness. We see kindnesses abounding as He empowers the strong to help with cleanup efforts in countries devastated by natural disasters.

Our Father God empowers us to lend a listening ear and assigns speakers of hope to walk the journey along with victims of abuse. By His grace and tender love, often manifested through His representatives here below, He gently lifts the weary, the downtrodden, and the grief-stricken, instilling hope where there was only despair. He beckons with the haunting melody of His call, "Come unto Me, all ye who are weary and heavy laden and I will give you rest." *In Christ we have the revelation of God's incarnation. He is indeed, and ever, with us.*

His everlasting arms are underneath and around us, upholding us. A mysterious grace-song was sung over me, just as He witnessed, and shared in, the tears and the lament poured out over our soldier-son who died too early.

I sense His Presence when I stand beside David's grave, when I see *Gentle-Warrior* etched there in the stone. The same One who wept with Mary when her brother Lazarus died weeps with me. He sings His grace-song over me, even as He affords me the space and place to grieve and lament my son, and He does so without hurrying me along. My comfort is in His holy, sacred, longsuffering Presence.

The grace-song is His Presence in the midst of a pain so profound. As I wrestled with my faith and flailed about, He did not shame, disregard, or give up on me.

I am not on the other side of my grief, but I do know myself to be in a different place, in which I am experiencing the early iterations of deep inner healing. His powerful touch has changed my life profoundly. I will always grieve my son's early death. I will grieve him when he isn't here to meet his nephews and nieces or to tease his sister—or marry and father children of his own. I will grieve him when we hang Christmas stockings and place his special ornament on the tree. I will grieve him when I hear Johnny Cash played and remember endless games of cards with "Folsom Blues" playing in the background. I will grieve him when I hear of war and bombings and of mothers grieving their children lost to the conflict. I will grieve him when he isn't here to comfort Jordan, his childhood friend—Jordan, who once listened to David for hours on end as he mourned the impending death of his grandmother. And now that friend, a courageous and authentic griever himself, laments the early cancer death of his beloved wife.

When I think of David's death, or the death of his friend's wife, or that of a teacher facing a classroom of six-year-olds, I am angry—justifiably so, I believe. I am angry at death, the enemy that destroys, all the while knowing that death itself, already mortally wounded but still in its own prolonged death throes, will be the last enemy to be destroyed, according to 1 Corinthians 15:25–26: "For He must reign until He has put all His enemies under His feet. The last enemy to be abolished is death." The original intention of the Author of Life was for life everlasting, and He will ultimately destroy death and the purposes of the enemy to destroy us and devastate our faith in a good God.

I am angry at the enemy's attempts to destroy our faith, by tactics like taking our loved ones in war, through cancer, and through violence. Although the enemy's intent is to destroy, the redemption story is both overriding and deeper. We live in a broken, messed up world, and it's the intent of the enemy to keep destroying, robbing, and killing. The beauty in our stories, though evil has indeed ravaged us, is redemption and a hope that is infinitely more powerful than any evil attempts to leave us in despair.

The enemy may think himself triumphant when death ensues, but the Lord brings us home.

I have been marked with a deep and hideous wound. But my wound doesn't gain the upper hand, doesn't speak more forcefully or with a stronger voice than the songs of redemption sung in triumph over me. Clearer and stronger than the most horrendous wound is the grace of God, brilliantly shining through all the broken places in my life, twinkling as it reflects off the shards of grief. For I know that He is with me, in every painful place, just as He has promised.

Four years before David died my friend Blythe and I were praying with a woman we had just met at the yearly prayer summit we attended in Cannon Beach, Oregon. We sat in a small circle to share a little about ourselves and then to pray together. Blythe and I knew each other well. We were friends who had also worked together at the same small church in Portland. Our children, too, were friends. She was acutely aware of my struggles with the nerve disorder and my relentless pain. Our new friend barely knew more about us than our names and the sketchy detail of the brief introductions in the small group. She later reported, however, that as she began to intercede on my behalf she saw me as a beautiful glass vase that, though full of hairline cracks, remained completely and remarkably intact. It was through those cracks, she shared, that God was brilliantly shining.

My dear, longtime friend and I glanced at each other with eyes filled with wonder: our new friend hadn't yet been aware of the intensity of physical pain in my life. We were both profoundly moved by the Lord's intimate awareness of my circumstances, as well as by His communication through this new acquaintance of what sounded like a song of grace over me. I lacked the power within myself to shine with His beauty in the midst of pain. It could be only through God's power and grace that the cracks in my life would be etched and outlined with the light of His glory.

The finding of my voice is in the telling of these stories. With my voice I narrate the stories of the hideous wound, of the deep grief of a son's violent death in Iraq. I tell the stories of how the Lord has shown up and how He has broken through my deep grief with His healing balm. I stand as a testament to His goodness and grace in the midst of deep sorrow and lament. The Father of mercies and the God of all comfort is indeed good.

There are times when I am not attuned to His voice; obstacles have usurped the melody for a season. Gravity has weighed me down, pulling my eyes ground-ward and bowing my head as the all-encompassing darkness of grief sets in. The experience is one of grief upon grief. I cannot comprehend or understand the "whys" of the suffering. *It doesn't make sense*, I cry out. Simplistic answers and pious platitudes bring little relief in this broken, diseased, and polluted world in which we grope for meaning.

This is the time for the cry of lament. The time to cry out to the God who pledges never to forsake us, to plead for His mercy as we traverse the road of grief, to implore Him for eyes to recognize His Presence in the midst of it all. It is in the pleading, in the cry of lament, that I reconnect with the One whose everlasting arms underpin me, promising His presence at all times and offering hope and healing for the asking.

Even as we weep He holds us in His arms and with His hands—those holy hands that carry the marks, His wounds. And He weeps with us, His tears intermingled with the strains of the grace-songs He sings over us.

War, cancer, and violence may kill and destroy, but the Lord brings us home. That is His beautiful redemption story, replete with hope. And it is in this that my hope rests and abides. God of Mystery, indeed.

How do we find our way in grief? How do we navigate through our losses and pain? What do we do when the weight of grief comes crashing through our ceilings and presses us to the ground so that we are powerless to so much as move on our own? I was helpless without God. But with His strength and encouragement I managed to take one step at a time, to get up out of bed, to work hard to face my grief. My broken story pointed to how desperately

I needed Him; my own story convinced me that I couldn't be strong on my own.

I needed Him then.

I need Him now.

I need Him.

I need Him every day of my life without my son. I need him as I live with this still so new dynamic within our family structure. I need Him when it feels too heavy, at times, to rebuild relationships within our family. I needed Him desperately when Jason completed his responsibilities with the Marines and then reenlisted with the Oregon National Guard, joining the same unit in which David had served. What was his mindset at the time? I was angry, confused, and fearful. What if he were deployed again? That day did come, and I was angry and terrified as he prepared to return for another tour in Iraq. Governor Kulongoski personally assured us that Jason would be assigned to a "safe" position, inside the wire. I was aghast that we were going through this again.

Jason returned to us safe. I was nearly undone during his second deployment, helpless as I was to control or countermand the decisions my adult son had made, or to understand his reasoning. Indeed, I needed Jesus.

I need Him still.

I need Him when each grandbaby is born, and they grow old enough to ask about Uncle David and why they can't meet him and play with him. I need Jesus when a grandson sobs in his Papa's arms, "I never met Uncle David, but I miss him." I need Jesus when another birthday passes and I wonder what David's life would have looked like at the age of thirty-six. I need Jesus when I bring out the Christmas decorations and my eyes fall on David's stocking, the one made of felt with the Nutcracker soldier. I need Jesus when I hear of family celebrations with entire families intact and when, in the hearing, I'm left breathless with remembering the hideous wound.

I need Him.

Jesus is my hope, the One who sings His grace-songs over me, who whispers in my ear of His love and presence.

I cannot begin to understand the presence of suffering and deep sorrow or explain why it is that God can seem aloof to the pain in this world. Nor will I try to posit an explanation, knowing it could never satisfy or be adequate.

What I can offer is my prayer of lament. I can unashamedly cry out to Him in a language He taught me, and I can confidently believe He will hear my cry. In faith, I lament to a God whom I believe—who I *know*—is with me and hears me. He may not answer in the ways I desire or expect. But I know and believe He hears my lament, just as He heard the biblical Jeremiah's and David's, . . . and Jesus'. I know and believe that He is with me as He was with them.

In lament, I offer my true self to the One whom I know to be present with us in all our suffering. And as I quiet myself and leave my lament with Him, I become attuned to his grace-song over me, to His healing balm being poured out, bringing peace in the midst of the storm.

As I sense the outpouring of God's healing balm, as I feel the soothing effects of His aloe on my burning skin, my lament takes a turn toward praise and gratefulness. Hope for healing has risen out of the ashes of despair, as healing and wholeness have been woven into the very fabric of my life. God has marked my life, my story, with redemption, hope, and healing more powerful by far than any wounds.

Mine is a beautiful, painful dance, but I don't dance alone. His everlasting arms are holding me, His peaceful presence surrounds me.

When my angst over David's passing reached its peak, my heart poured out a lament, a prayer, an offering. As I wrestled with my pain and poured out my sorrow, the Lord poured in to me a grace-song. It was a sacred gift, unexpected.

I was finding my voice again. A new language was being birthed in my heart and spilling out from my lips.

*Marilyn's Lament*

*"O Lord, I plead with You, hear my cry.*
*Sorrow upon sorrow has led me to the shadowlands.*
*My body deteriorates while my soul languishes.*
*Heartache upon heartache, I can hardly breathe.*
*Shallow breaths I take and a sob once again pours*
*forth into another torrent of tears,*
*tears of heart, soul and mind, crushed, bruised.*
*Silent, how silent You seem.*
*Alone with my grief,*

*time passes as the raw retching spills out again.*
*I'm waiting! For how long will I wait?*
*I demand! I sorrow! I fear! I rage!*
*Strength departed, too tired to fight.*
*Will You rescue me? Will You save me?*
*Light, I see it through the grievous thick, dark fog.*
*Faithful and amazingly patient.*
*Oftentimes I am too tired to hear, to see, to touch.*
*Now I see as You uncover and reveal amazing*
*longsuffering and love.*
*Bulletproof love, endless, bottomless erosion-free,*
*uncomplicated.*
*You've never left.*
*You wait.*
*I cannot see clearly through this mourning*
*mother's heart.*
*What I can see is light and beautiful.*
*What I can hear is their prayers,*
*Your word, her counsel.*
*What I can feel is their hands laid on me*
*and You are pulsating through with Resurrection*
*life, uncovering Redemption.*
*Hope springs forth.*
*It seems so odd to feel hopeful*
*when the pain, suffering and suffocating truth*
*remain unchanged and I feel betrayed.*
*He is gone.*
*My body crumbles.*

*I could laugh and mock and cynically throw it all*
*on You, blaming You.*
*I could harden my heart.*
*You pursue.*
*Your Hand is firm on me.*
*You whisper peace.*
*You whisper comfort.*
*You lavish me with grace!*
*This madness may not change, ah, but neither*
*does Your Love!*
*But in fact, in truth: Your love is never ending.*
*And I have the promise of heaven.*
*And someday I will dance.*
*And someday I will dance with him.*
*And what I lament will no longer be lamented.*
*I will wait with hope.*
*Shepherd, I invite You to come and carry me in Your*
*strong, healing, comforting Arms of peace and love.*

# Chapter 20

# Connection

At David's burial service, when the Gold Star mom dressed in white formally spoke to me on bended knee and presented me with a Gold Star pin, we connected.

I don't recall her name, and most of what she said to me was a blur of words. I do remember her voice speaking over me words I would never have expected to hear. I'd never expected to join this particular group of mothers, and yet here I was receiving into my hand the symbol of that which connected us. At the time I wanted to refuse her presence, resist her words, and float away, though I found myself drawn to her tender, knowing gaze and earnest words.

This exclusive club of which I am now a part never sends invitations; still, when I joined I was met with open arms. She knew. I was sure she knew the pain in my heart.

Years later, as I thumbed through the *TAPS* magazine, my eyes landed once again on the list of events and retreats the group provide for survivors. *TAPS* stands for Tragedy Assistance Program for Survivors. A description on their website states: "The Tragedy Assistance Program for Survivors offers compassionate care to all those grieving the death of a loved one serving in our Armed Forces. Since 1994, TAPS has provided comfort and hope 24 hours a day, seven days a week through a national peer support network and connection to grief resources, all at no cost to surviving families and loved ones."

I learned that TAPS provides a myriad of events, including camps, seminars, retreats, and expeditions for family members. Today my eyes landed on the Mom's Retreat, to be held in February at the Islandwood Retreat Center on Bainbridge Island in the Puget Sound, roughly three hours from where I lived. I noted the sign-up date and decided it was time. I had been pushing aside these invitations to participate, not wanting to be exposed and vulnerable with strangers. I chuckled to myself over this reservation now; after all, everyone participating would be coming with like fears and concerns. In all likelihood the majority of the group would be struggling with fears about being vulnerable with strangers.

A friend whom I had met on the first Veteran's Day after David's death traveled with me to Bainbridge Island. She drove, which nixed my plan to escape in my car in the case of vulnerability overload. We talked all the way there about our sons, Chase and David. The atmosphere was easy and comfortable, as we had by this time known each other for years. Uncertain what to expect when we arrived, I felt anxiety creeping in. My friend, however, who had attended several TAPS events and volunteered for the organization as a peer mentor, was relaxed and calm.

We were met by two of the leaders, whose kind smiles put me at ease. They grabbed all of our luggage, placing it in a large wheelbarrow before heading down the path to place it in our room. Before leaving, they directed us to the registration table in the conference center.

I felt shy as we entered the room but soon found myself put at ease once again by kindness and ready smiles. Later, after everyone had arrived, we gathered in the main meeting room where there was a roaring fire, chairs positioned in a circle, and tables set up for art projects. The weekend promised us times of creativity, rest, hiking, and yoga, as well as the sharing of stories and the making of new friends.

After we had spent some time introducing ourselves, we were given an opportunity to share our stories. There were twenty-four mothers in attendance, all of whom had lost sons. We represented a cross-section of the population, identifying ourselves as teachers, a librarian, an office manager, a physician's assistant, a broker, a school bus driver, a quilter, and several stay-at-home moms. In addition, we represented various belief systems and manifested unique personalities. A common thread wove us together, however, as we shared our stories: we were grieving mamas, a great leveler. Our personal and professional lives weren't of great import; what we collectively shared was of the upmost priority.

We all listened attentively to one another, holding space for each story to be told. A bond like no other was being formed among us as we spoke of our deepest heartache and connected over our shared sorrows. Our leaders watched over us and led our group well, offering enriching activities, and deep conversations ensued. Throughout the entire event I never felt as though I needed to escape. By the end of our four days together on Bainbridge Island, we felt like forever friends. Living as we do all over the country, we decided to stay connected using a private Facebook page. We took extra measures to jointly connect on our sons' birthdays, as well as on the anniversaries of their deaths. Still today, when we are sad and struggling we oftentimes reach out to one another. We are sister-friends.

Months later I had the opportunity to consider additional involvement with TAPS. The email inviting me to attend the November 2016 Remembrance Day events in London arrived on my birthday in May. I was trembling with excitement and delight as Jim and I talked about the possibility of my attending. We decided that this would be the trip of a lifetime, and I applied for the London trip in November.

The time spent in London far exceeded my expectations. We were included in many Remembrance Day events, and numerous activities had been planned and organized by TAPS. I was impressed by how effectively the British honor their veterans and war dead. Events were scheduled for four days. These included parades on the River Thames, another parade that wound through the city, a fireworks display, the laying of wreaths on the Cenotaph by the Queen, and a veterans' parade that featured men and women from all over the United Kingdom, as well as families of the fallen. I watched Prince Charles from about fifty yards away as he saluted each group marching past him in the veterans' parade. All of these events were open to the public and well attended. There were also televised private events attended by only the royal family and public officials. The atmosphere surrounding all of these was somber, sacred, and very respectful. As we wandered the streets of London we noticed that the majority of the British wear red poppies on their lapels throughout the month of November to remember those who have given their lives.

There were thirty-six TAPS participants from all over the United States who had flown in for the London events. Widows, brothers, sisters, mothers, and fathers arrived as strangers who would soon become friends. At our first meeting a lengthy block of time was set aside for the sacred stories to be told. One by one the most courageous men and women I've ever met stood and spoke about the loss of their loved ones. Again we held space for each one—space for honoring each name and each face, space to commemorate these precious loved ones who were no longer with us, gone too soon. I don't recall how long it took for each story to be spoken. What I do remember is how beautiful it was for us to listen together, sharing tears, sorrows, and knowing nods. Love, respect, and honor were conferred and received in that conference room at the Crown Plaza in London. We made space for one another from the first day we met, and all alike relished this safe place to be vulnerable and share our deepest sorrows. Both individually and collectively we had been marked, indelibly, by loss. Now lifelong friendships were being forged from the ashes. It was a privilege to hear these stories, and I felt exhausted with emotion afterward.

We were given wooden crosses, each adorned with a red poppy. on the first day we gathered as a group. Each of us was invited to write our loved one's name on our cross, along with anything else we desired—perhaps a verse, a poem, or a date. We were to take our crosses to the Westminster Abbey Field of Remembrance and place them in the ground in the designated area for the fallen from the United States. When we arrived and walked to the area marked out for us, we huddled together and stared. All around in the garden were thousands of crosses already placed in the ground in memory of the fallen from many years and many battles. There was sufficient space for all of the allies of the United Kingdom to place their crosses, each bearing the name of a love one. A hush overtook us as we waited to begin. Here was yet another sacred space to hold our stories and to remember and honor our fallen warriors. Several young widows in our group took the initiative to begin placing their crosses, one by one, in the cold, hard earth. We stood with silent tears coursing down our cheeks, watching these brave souls honoring their deceased husbands. Each of us, singly, took the time we needed. Space was allowed, the need for it understood. This was holy ground. It took my breath away.

After placing our crosses in the gardens, several of us were given a private tour of the grounds surrounding

Westminster Abbey. As our tour came to a close we stood together on a corner behind the British Parliament buildings and Big Ben. The sun was setting, and there was an intense golden glow from the tower. Pausing in our tracks, we were mesmerized by the sight of a rainbow painted in the skies above. We captured the stunning moment on our iPhones and continued standing in wonder, our faces upturned. I felt as though the Lord were saying "I see you. I see your pain, and I am with you."

The following day we participated in yet another deeply meaningful event, the Silence in the Square of Armistice Day, November 11, in Trafalgar Square. We arrived early for the ceremony, to be hosted by the Royal British Legion, and it included a variety of musical renditions, poems, and other readings. The public square at the base of the National Gallery was filled with people, both locals and travelers; a large group of Scottish veterans in their berets and kilts stood to our right.

Trafalgar Square, located in the heart of the city, has been a significant landmark since the thirteenth century. A 169-foot granite column, with the statue of Admiral Horatio Nelson atop, stands at the center, guarded by four enormous lion statues and flanked by two large fountains on either side. This is one of the busiest places in London, with continuous movement of people, taxis, buses, and bicycles. On this particular day—on the eleventh day of the eleventh month at precisely 11:11 a.m.—the square, as well as the entire United Kingdom, falls silent for two minutes in memory of the men and women who have sacrificed their lives in the great war, as well as for all who have died in combat since that time.

After the hour-long program a mournful song was sung, without accompaniment, immediately prior to the beginning of the two minutes of silence. Its ending would serve as the cue for the silence to commence. We stood reverently as the sad song drew to a close, . . . and then there was utter silence in London. We watched from the stairs of the National Gallery as the pedestrians stopped in their tracks. As the taxis, buses, and bicyclists came to a halt. No horns blared, not a word was spoken; there were only the sounds of the birds in the air.

For two holy minutes the city of London stood still and at attention, collectively remembering and honoring. The experience was astounding—clearly one of the most sacred moments in my life. I was deeply moved as this great city paused to pay tribute.

Afterward we were given handfuls of paper poppy petals to throw into the aqua waters of the enormous fountains. Our group gathered as one, simultaneously tossing in the red petals—a holy gesture of remembering. As the poppies began to fill the fountains, I was sobered by the remembering—by the music, the poetry, the poppies, the people, . . . and, most of all, the silence. The marque event on this day struck a deep cord in me. This is a memory I will always hold close to my heart. Thank you, London.

And thank you, Tragedy Assistance Program for

Survivors. This organization, unlike any other I've known, provides unique opportunities for families, offering space to share stories, connect, and forge lifelong friendships. We have all been through deep waters, many of us losing family members due to the violence of war. TAPS offers sorely needed support and understanding as we navigate our grief. I have experienced a new level of healing, hope, and wholeness as I've participated in the events this organization has graciously offered. I am grateful for the friendships made and for the compassionate love that has been shared. I am grateful for connection.

Chapter 21

# Family

Three grandsons giggled in my garden one afternoon when they were preschoolers. Together they straddled a downed cottonwood, as though bound for a journey on this unlikely conveyance. The oldest shouted something about traveling to Oklahoma. Quickly joining the bandwagon, his twin cousins called out to me in laughter, "Meme, we're going to Oklahoma!" Another burst of giggles morphed into belly laughs as they waved goodbye and took off on their journey. The younger two would do and say nearly everything their deeply admired older cousin suggested.

Their unrestrained belly laughs would get me every time. I suspected in this particular instance that their exuberance was brought on, at least in part, by a birthday tradition in our family. It was David's birthday, and he had always requested my frozen mocha cheesecake for his celebration. We now enjoy it as a family every year as we remember his birth and life—as we share memories of a son, brother, brother-in-law, and uncle, gone too soon.

The cousins licked their plates until every last hint of the chocolate goodness had been eradicated. Our oldest grandson jumped down to run outside, his admiring cousins following suit, as always. They didn't have time for Meme to clean their faces. They were on a mission.

The boys ran freely in the garden, happily frolicking together and planning adventures on this warm day in May, while their daddies were building a new addition to our deck. Their bursts of shrill laughter punctuated and rose above the intermittent blasts of drilling and hammering. These boys mirror my own three sons, the younger two also being twin boys.

I tried to capture these moments in photographs, snapping picture after picture, loath to miss one moment. Then I stopped, tucked the camera in my pocket, and practiced presence. I drank in the joyful, chocolate-kissed faces; the contagious laughter; the friendly banter; and the boundless, and now undoubtedly chocolate-fueled, energy.

He would have embraced every moment watching those messy-faced boys playing with such abandon. My David had loved children and would have relished his role as an uncle, most certainly moving from spectator to participant. As I began to think about his childhood ways, I was jolted back to the present as my grandsons clamored for my attention. "Look at the rocks we found in Oklahoma, Meme!"

I've made the choice to be intentionally present when my grandchildren visit, though I'm often beckoned back to another time by a jolting déjà vu insinuated upon the scene by memories of my own little ones. An ongoing, if lower key, level of grief over my son's early death has a way of overriding almost any other thought I ponder. Memories can be triggered at any time and in any place. On this day I adjusted my eyes toward the living, though tears slid quietly from the corners of my eyes. I deliberately slammed shut the door on that unbidden recollection of two soldiers bearing an unwelcome revelation. I reminded myself to breathe and relived the beauty of that special beach in Maui.

Earlier in the day my grandchildren had blown out the candles on David's birthday dessert. We had sung "Happy Birthday" to Uncle David, celebrating his life. I had once again fought back the urge to scream out my hatred of war and death, pain and suffering, as we adults, his parents and siblings, choked out the words of the birthday song. No, I hadn't birthed my son to send him off to fight and die in a faraway war. How does one, afterward, mark the day of his birth and honor his life? Elizabeth suggested discreetly that singing "Happy Birthday" might have been a little over the top. Perhaps next year we'll substitute colorful balloons to mark the day of his birth, writing messages on them and releasing them skyward. David would appreciate that gesture. And we'll always savor that frozen mocha cheesecake.

Eyes met across the kitchen, the eyes of older parents remembering their own little ones sitting around our kitchen table, singing birthday songs and celebrating. A much different, gentler world had been ours.

We smiled tenderly as we gazed at our grandchildren. We often glimpse David in their dancing eyes, mischievous smiles, serious tones, exuberant laughter, . . . and love for frozen mocha cheesecake. We joined in the merriment as they licked their plates clean, hopped off their chairs, and headed once again for Oklahoma on a downed cottonwood, laughing heartily. Aubie, our solicitous granddaughter, is concerned about whether our talk of David might have made me sad. I am deeply touched by her sensitivity at such a young age.

Plans were being formulated to celebrate my own sixtieth birthday only two weeks later. An epic celebration, in fact, was in the works. *Epic* in my world equated to inviting about thirty of my dearest girlfriends and family members to a dance party on our deck. A large white tent was to cover the deck, overlooking the golf course. A DJ had been hired, and I intended to dance all night.

Unbeknownst to me, a few days before my party two young friends from church had a surprise birthday outing planned. They picked me up at a restaurant in Northeast Portland where I was having dinner with another friend from church. "Here's the plan, Marilyn . . . You've been talking about getting a nose piercing, and the day has come! You have an appointment in less than thirty minutes, and we're taking you there now!" Having time neither to think nor protest, I was excited and also a little jittery. They took me to a place on Glisan Street called The Black Hole, and I was so out of my element. Emily Rose would do the honors. I chose the jewelry, and up the stairs I climbed to finally get a nose piercing after ten years of talking about it. My friends took pictures during the entire process, as I grimaced and giggled. Then, later in the week, we did indeed dance for hours at my lovely, lively party hosted by Elizabeth and Adina and complete with food and flowers, music, dancing, and a s'mores station at the fire pit. My eighty-year-old friend who had traveled to England with me cut up the dance floor, while my youngest personal friend flirted with the handsome DJ. Jim and Barry served us drinks and kept the fire pit blazing, while Barry snuck onto the dance floor for a quick spin with my eighty-year-old friend, much to everyone's delight.

We danced with abandon, my women friends and I, one of whom declared this to be the most fun she had ever had at a birthday party. I celebrated the day of my birth by being fully present among the loveliest of friends, many of whom had walked gently beside me during my darkest days. Others, newer friends, embraced our friendship and honored me well.

I gratefully celebrated my restored health, as well as the forgiveness that had replaced resentment toward those who had terminated my career in youth ministry. I gratefully celebrated those surrounding me on the dance floor—very much including those who had held space for me as I walked the journey of grief, those who had listened and wept and honored. Elizabeth honored me with a speech exuding love and affection, yet another grace-song sung over me. These were women who had championed me while I learned a new language and found my voice in a new way. They now surrounded me with love and laughter and the deepest joy. My heart could have burst with gratefulness at being so loved.

Weeks later Jim spoke about getting a tattoo. We were having dinner with some friends, and he described the tattoo in detail, obviously having given the idea careful thought. He explained what he envisioned: a family tree, its actual form that of an oak. The trunk was to consist of two separate portions twisted together, symbolizing our marriage. There would be four main branches, representing all four of our children, as well as five smaller branches stemming from two of them, representing our grandchildren.

Our friends asked about our children and grandchildren. We were just getting to know this couple, and they were unfamiliar with our family. Jim painted the picture with a broad stroke: "All of our surviving children are married and live in the Portland metro area." Our friends encouraged him to describe them in greater detail.

Elizabeth, our oldest, is a heart nurse at a Portland hospital. She also volunteers with Compassion Connect and at the local grade school where her boys attend. She is humble and compassionate. Her husband, Erik, is in property management, along with his parents. He started a nonprofit for at-risk youth and is also an artist. After David's death Erik composed and painted a picture of Elizabeth's courage as she faced her grief. The painting is of a lion on a mountain, facing a deep crevice. It still stands as one of my favorite paintings. Erik is patient and creative. Elizabeth and Erik have twin sons who are in the first grade. Silas has a sharp wit and weaves amazing stories. He also loves to swim. Elliott is full of wonder, tenderhearted, and skilled in constructing elaborate Lego creations the average twelve-year-old would be proud of having built. He plays the violin. Both love to read.

Jason, who loves working with his hands and is by nature selfless and sacrificial, is a foreman for a construction company that builds homes east of Portland. He also started making artistic signs out of re-claimed wood, enjoying the creative side of himself. His wife, Cindy, is a pharmacy technician employed near their home. Cindy particularly adores her sister's girls and would do anything in the world for them. They love dogs, the Oregon State Beavers, and Cindy's two little nieces—though not necessarily in that order.

Daniel is a 911 dispatcher for Multnomah County who also volunteers for the Clackamas Fire Department. Daniel is steady and calm and has a crazy sense of humor. He enjoys playing a variety of instruments, especially the drums. Adina, a teacher by profession, currently provides daycare in her home while raising the couple's three children. Adina sings beautifully and has boundless energy. Daniel and Adina both participate on a worship team at their church. Their older daughter, Aubie, who is in the fourth grade, loves art and animals and is interested in trying out every imaginable sport—her passion currently is basketball. Lincoln David is in the second grade and is smart and creative; he particularly enjoys reading and dreams of traveling with Meme to London and Paris. He also loves his new gymnastics class, especially the rings. Quinnleigh, at three, is full of spunk. She adores her new puppy and especially loves to wear princess dresses and perform a dance and song rendition of "Let It Go" whenever the family gathers. She changes into different princess dresses about ten times a day.

Our friends asked us to tell them a little about David, and we were happy to oblige.

David was noble, kind, brave, and equipped with a particularly dry sense of humor. He loved his friends and family, as well as children in general; he would have adored his two nieces and three nephews. He regularly brought me flowers and would have done anything for the men he served alongside in Iraq. He hated the war and didn't believe in it, though he kept his promise to serve because he had taken an oath. David was a gentle warrior. He had never had an opportunity to marry or to father children of his own.

When we began discussing the tattoo again, I found myself quiet and agitated, though I wasn't exactly sure why. After we had returned home, climbed into bed, and turned off the lamps on our nightstands, I lay awake for hours. What was troubling me about the tattoo? It wasn't about the tattoo itself, I was certain; I was fine with Jim getting one, if that's what he wanted to do.

It was about the branches, so full of life, and most particularly the one representing David. Because it was empty of offshoots. When I thought about that empty branch quiet tears began streaming down my face. I wept for what could have been, had his life not been cut short. I wept for his missed opportunity to be a husband and father. I wept for the grandchildren I would never hold, those to whom I would never read his favorite childhood books that I had saved. I wept for the missed trips to Disneyland, to the park, or to the beach. I wept over his missed opportunities to play with his nieces and nephews and to sing "Happy Birthday" to them. I wept for him—for what might have been in his life—again and again and again as fresh waves of grief crashed against me that night.

At times I feel as though the work of grief is nearly finished. Then another anniversary passes and another layer is exposed. It seems that there is always more to mourn, to lament, to work through.

Negotiating grief isn't a simple process, progressing neatly from one stage to another. It isn't a once and for all proposition. But those ups and downs and backs and forths are to be expected. Too often those who love us want to hurry us along through the process. It is almost as though I can feel their impatience simmering. We all grieve and process differently, and this variation can be terribly uncomfortable for those looking on. It can be uncomfortable for churchgoers who want to mollify us with quick and easy answers and send us on our way, restored and healed. But religious platitudes and clichés are anything but helpful when addressed to a broken heart. I think about God's original design for His creation. As the Author of life, He designed us to do just that: live. It has never been His intention for any of us to be taken out by an airliner speeding into a skyscraper, a gunman decimating a classroom of six-year-olds, an IED, or cancer. Death is the last enemy that will be defeated. In His grace and goodness our Father redeems our death and brings us home to heaven.

Will I ever be on the other side of my own grief story? Sometimes I'm doing well for a long period of time, and then . . .

It's the anniversary of 9/11, and I find myself flat on my face. I imagine the collective cries of the thousands who have mourned the deaths of the ones they loved, the ones brutally killed. I see the flags at half-staff. Friends bring flowers and words written on a card, remembering. I hear read aloud the names of innocent victims, struck down on that terrible day.

Two days later, on September 13, comes another anniversary, more poignant for us by far because it marks *his* death. Jim and I make our way around Mount Scott, fresh flowers from our garden in hand, to Willamette National Cemetery. His grave is there, in Section X, *Gentle Warrior* etched in the granite stone.

Silent, we hold each other close as tears roll unimpeded down our faces. Last year we stood here and heard Taps being played in the distance, around the bend after the graveside service of an older veteran. The sound waves wove their way through the acres of green until they reached our ears. We stood on the sacred hill, quiet, sensing the Presence of God surrounding, embracing, and comforting.

We miss you, son! Oh, how we miss you! We miss your smile and your laughter. We miss your presence with our family. We love you! Oh, how we love you! This missing is always with us, unchanging in its meaning and intensity.

We drive away, toward our grandchildren who were gathered at Elizabeth's home and enjoying one another's company on the anniversary of his death. As soon as we arrive and begin to walk up to the house, we hear the delighted giggles of three little boys. They are running in and out of our daughter's home in circular motion.

Lincoln David in the lead, Elliott and Silas follow their older cousin. We watch them running and hear their laughter, sensing their joy in being together. Glad smiles welcome us, arms open wide, hugs and sloppy kisses, joyful greetings.

And, in the air, I detect the echoes of another's laughter . . .

# Acknowledgments

I am brimming with gratefulness to my publisher, Tim Beals, and the Credo House Publishers team, for believing in me and making me an author. Many thanks to Tim and his staff for helping me navigate a territory new to me, with your expert advice and leading. I am also tremendously grateful for my editor, Donna Huisjen, for her skillfulness, insight, and thoughtfulness.

Author and friend Leslie Gould, you have been my coach, writing mentor, and one who has championed me early on to write my story. Leslie, I don't believe this book would have materialized without you. My gratefulness abounds to you, my friend.

To my early readers, Blythe Nordbye and Kathy Crannell: thank you for your commitment, guidance, prayers, support, and encouragement.

To Renee Naslund, thank you for reading and carefully observing those troublesome grammatical errors and kindly helping me make my manuscript presentable.

To Rhonda, Jody, Kathleen, and Amy, thank you for meeting on Mondays all those years ago, to pray for our loved ones serving in Iraq.

To my counselor, Cindy Brosh, thank you for your compassion, insight, care, and strength and for pointing me toward hope. You believed in the fruition of this book before I believed it was possible.

To Nancy Linnon, my gifted writing coach and our Wednesday morning writing group, thank you for holding space for me and listening well.

To my friend Carmen VanEck, for your gentle, consistent encouragement and belief in me. Thank you for introducing me to your dad, Tim Beals, who, unbeknownst to me, happened to be in the publishing business.

To the Schlesinger family, thank you for creating and supporting The David Weisenburg Memorial Scholarship at Portland State University.

To the President and Founder of TAPS (Tragedy Assistance Program for Survivors), Bonnie Carroll, thank you for your vision and the formation of TAPS for all the family members who have loved ones who have died while in the military. Thank you, Bonnie, for creating a space built for support, deep connection, and further healing.

To Pastors Rick McKinley, Heather Thomas, Josh Butler, and Ben Thomas for your inspiration and encouragement to write my story.

To all the women in my grief groups at Imago Dei Community Church, you are all women of courage and valor. It has been a tremendous privilege to hear your stories and call you friends.

Finally, to my husband, Jim, my children and my grandchildren, and my sister, Julie, thank you for loving me and supporting me throughout this process. Much love to you all!